Resilience Across Spectrum Engineering Workforce

Resilience Across Spectrums for the Engineering Workforce

Claudia Rose BA, MAIT
Kim Idol PhD
Ellen Birrell MA

𝒞𝒲𝒫

Central West Publishing

Disclaimer
Every effort has been made by the publisher, editors and authors while preparing this book, however, no warranties are made regarding the accuracy and completeness of the content. The publisher, editors and authors disclaim without any limitation all warranties as well as any implied warranties about sales, along with fitness of the content for a particular purpose. Citation of any website and other information sources does not mean any endorsement from the publisher, editors and authors. For ascertaining the suitability of the contents contained herein for a particular lab or commercial use, consultation with the subject expert is needed. In addition, while using the information and methods contained herein, the practitioners and researchers need to be mindful for their own safety, along with the safety of others, including the professional parties and premises for whom they have professional responsibility. To the fullest extent of law, the publisher, editors and authors are not liable in all circumstances (special, incidental, and consequential) for any injury and/or damage to persons and property, along with any potential loss of profit and other commercial damages due to the use of any methods, products, guidelines, procedures contained in the material herein.

NATIONAL LIBRARY OF AUSTRALIA

A catalogue record for this book is available from the National Library of Australia

ISBN (print): 978-1-922617-33-0

About the Book

To create a community that remains productive and competitive, our society needs to foster individual and organizational changes. We need to develop an adaptive mindset in individuals and foster organizational agility. With this attitude, organizations and individuals can encourage the workforce to adapt to changing forces and continue to support their organization despite the systemic issues and the emotional challenges posed by existent personal, professional, and even spiritual conflicts,

Resilience is our name for this adaptive mindset; it is the ability to survive difficulties and strengthen this adaptive faculty. It is the developed ability to perceive changes in circumstances and confidently modify behaviors to maximize positive outcomes. It is the ability to thrive by developing new coping skills and strengths. The result is a positive, flexible reaction to large and small changes in the system, the environment, and the society of people and entities involved in the creative process.

Claudia Rose BA, MAIT
Kim Idol PhD
Ellen Birrell MA

Acknowledgments

We would like to thank several groups and individuals who played a significant role in helping shape and test the ideas in this book by offering their expertise in service of this project.

We would like to the members of the NDIA Architecture Subcommittee for vetting this project and offering several additional examples to flesh out the training protocols. We would also like to thank the INCOSE mini-conference members in San Diego who offered additional suggestions and comments as well as a place to present and test these ideas in real-world settings.

Most importantly we would like to acknowledge Audrey Thompson, an international executive coach and Michele NAME for attending innumerable brainstorming and refinement sessions in which they provided invaluable expertise and experience-based knowledge that helped refine the content as well as the training protocols in this book.

Table of Contents

1

The Modern American Workforce

New Realities

The modern American workforce has fundamentally changed over the years. In the 21st century, what supervisors, stockholders, consumers, and employees want in terms of productivity, loyalty, innovation, working conditions, recognition, and reward has changed. Today's engineering workforce team consists of an exceptionally diverse group in terms of life, work experience, and age, and these realities are reshaping the workplace.

The mix of long-term experienced, short-term and new employees, technologies, value systems, public pressures, and modes of production have altered the way employees behave under pressure. Complex organizations now test product development and regulate productivity in what would be considered inconceivable ways a decade ago. Sometimes this reality allows for new consumer goods and services to be produced in record time, but it can also reduce quality, stall invention, and impede progress.

Tenured employees sometimes feel loss and even grief or depression because it seems to them that their values and dedication are outdated and unappreciated or discarded. Meanwhile, younger generations entering the workforce seem to lack the ability to accept performance related criticism or accommodate failure as an inherent aspect of productivity and adaptation. With their focus on maintaining a balance between their professional and private lives, this younger generation prioritizes their personal lives differently than other generations do. They limit how much effort and time they contribute to projects in ways the more tenured employees do not. They also do not necessarily admire those who do what they refuse to do. One generation has a generally more comprehensive focus on the big picture.

In contrast, by virtue of training and socialization, others are determined experts focused on smaller pieces of the big picture. Innovation and creativity become stifled in the mix. Although there is a trend of generalizing cultural groups with shared ideologies that may conflict at work, there are also individuals involved in the workforce who do not fit into any established group culture. In addition, the current disruptions due to the Covid-19 pandemic and the likelihood of future epidemics create the demand for training in what we call resiliency.

To create a community that remains productive and competitive, our society needs to foster individual and organizational changes. We need to develop an adaptive mindset in individuals and foster organizational agility. With this attitude, organizations and individuals can encourage the workforce to adapt to changing forces and continue to support their organization despite the systemic issues and the emotional challenges posed by existent personal, professional, and even spiritual conflicts,

Resilience is our name for this adaptive mindset; it is the ability to survive difficulties and strengthen this adaptive faculty. It is the developed ability to perceive changes in circumstances and confidently modify behaviors to maximize positive outcomes. It is the ability to thrive by developing new coping skills and strengths. The result is a positive, flexible reaction to large and small changes in the system, the environment, and the society of people and entities involved in the creative process.

This skill set fosters the ability to thrive during challenging times, for extended periods (i.e., being quarantined and accepting social distancing as a new constant) and continue to adapt. Before Covid-19, many cultural and practical changes in the American workplace had already altered the way we acquired jobs, kept them, and determined whom we hired for open positions. A more systematic approach to changing was becoming necessary. Multiple "policies and procedures" were promulgated within organizations to ensure fair work practices with varying outcomes.

In general, all of us live longer and are able and often required to work longer. Discussions regarding raising the retirement age as a matter of economic necessity are no longer abstract. Human beings are living longer, *healthier* lives. Senior employees now bring energy, experience, and creativity to the workplace resulting from long-term experience. Technology is reducing some jobs and creating others. The way we do business is changing. What globalization means is going to change in the coming years. Our need to exploit opportunities and address the emergence of new demands now and in the foreseeable future also creates opportunities that demand adaptation.

Generations Apart, at Work, Together

The modern-day senior workforce must contend with long-standing assumptions of corporate culture that are, in fact, obsolete. It is common for older workers who are experienced and educated, employees with proven records of adjusting to changing market needs, to find themselves unhireable *because* of their experience and high skill levels. In theory, senior workers may expose employers to higher health costs. It is assumed they will be resistant to change, are 'behind" in technical mastery, and have expectations of high respect and salary. Many employers seek to avoid these potential costs by hiring a younger workforce. These younger workers are individuals who require more training, extensive mentoring and are a more labor intensive, expensive workforce in terms of management resources. This is where your authors have been called in to attempt to teach both basic skills and to transfer a depth of knowledge and systems mindset that is not accessible in an introductory skills course.

Senior workforce employees must overcome the bias that shapes their interactions with Human Resource (HR) departments. Companies must keep the HR departments updated on the current employment environment. To retain corporate knowledge and attract desirable new applicants, it is incumbent upon corporations to amend their definitions of a desirable employee. It is also incumbent upon senior workers to exercise emotional agility and emotional intelligence to combat established ageist ideologies without hostility but with resilience. They also need to cope with the inevitable feelings of exhaustion and depression that accompany the need to constantly reframe longevity so that it is understood as a positive aspect accentuating their skill sets and making them more saleable.

Luckily, older workers usually come equipped with some resilience. The older you are, the more likely you have recovered from several setbacks that inevitably occur as time passes. The 20-year-old fresh from college is less likely to have lost parents, a number of friends, suffered through changes in the industry or endured the financial or health setbacks an older individual will have experienced. Did you

3

lose your home in the last economic downturn? Did it burn down in the fires that swept through the west in the previous years? Did you divorce? Did your eyesight get worse? Has the career path you trained for altered or vanished, and how did you adapt when this happened? While we survive and recover from these events, they change our worldview. Maturity comes at a price, and while the benefits of learning through experience also make a more complex individual who is more likely to be a valuable employee, it can also combine with setbacks in terms of finding work. Outdated skill sets can darken one's point of view and prompt retreat. On a regular basis, you are more likely to be dealing with a serious personal setback as an older worker than a younger one, making job hunting harder.

Success in this situation requires a strong support network, an enduring sense of humor, and an ability to carry on through the days of resentment and sadness that accompanies experienced individuals as they try to master new ways of presenting themselves to those who need to hire them (though they can't see it yet). In sum, the modern workplace is an environment that requires acquisition of new behavioral standards and challenges value systems for all concerned.

Tribes on the Work Floor

Within organizations, people organize into sub-groups often referred to by Enterprise Architects as tribes. These tribes are composed of individuals who share common values and experiences and may feel the need to compete with other groups or tribes for resources. The other tribes within the changing workforce may be organized by their era of birth and training; they are known by nicknames: Millennials (Generation-Yers), Generation-Zers, Generation-Xers.

Each tribe has a commonly observed set of attributes that may not apply to the individuals but can describe some of the behaviors and paradigms of the group. The Generation-X group is described as a population that "... self-defines itself as being loyal, compassionate, thoughtful, open-minded, responsible, and determined" (Seemiller, 2016). Members of these groups judge their peers as competitive, spontaneous, adventuresome, and curious - characteristics that they do not see readily in themselves and that older workers profess they do not see in them (Seemiller, 2016). This younger group scores

4

lower in terms of reading competencies but higher in aptitudes concerning digital devices, platforms, and texts (Amiama-Espaillat & Mayor-Ruiz, 2017). Like their older counterparts, this group is characterized by a common understanding that their quality of life will likely plateau and deteriorate for them. Born into a world altered by terrorism (domestic and foreign) and regular economic recessions, their sense of progress is locked into the sense of inevitable economic constriction. These millennials (for the purposes of not naming all of these younger groups every time we discuss them) are having fewer children and having them later. Thus, there is no bulge of younger workers waiting to fill in the jobs as there once was. An older workforce is now a standard and necessary component of any successful business plan.

Americans are now commonly working into their 70s and 80s because they can or may have to. Only a small flush of younger employees wait at the gates to take over responsibilities. When the younger workers join the workforce, they often lack the job and life skills to thrive and survive in modern workforce situations. They are often burdened with debt in ways their older counterparts were not when they started out. College is a minimum standard of education for most, and the prices have gone up, grants have vanished, so a large student loan debt and credit debt to fund their lifestyles are common.

Generational Conflict

The convergence of two generational tribes of workers in an everyday workplace forces meaningful change and requires the development of empathy and communication. A sense of inclusive community is needed. Younger employees entering the workforce and older, more experienced, and valuable employees need to forge a common ground in terms of values and work ethic. More senior, skilled, and experienced members of the workforce feel threatened by the existence of a generation that seems to value freedom over employment and is threatened by those who insist on sacrificing freedom/family time/personal time for frangible employment opportunities. This new group also places a higher value on feelings than on accomplishment, more than members of the older group do. The pressures created by these conflicting perspectives require a means to evolve and adapt that lessens the perceived threats posed by "the others." This convergence of different groups and individuals requires a support-ive, adaptive environment. Thus, business enterprises need to foster positive changes in this emergent environment and implement a transparent positive value system that can drive successful adapta-tions and convergence. In other words, we need to develop a frame-work for a successful merge so that changing values support work products and workflow, which in turn will enrich individual and cor-poration interests.

New Strategies: Resilience Training

Rather than simply refusing to concede the assumption that no one is comfortable in the modern workforce, we need to learn workforce resilience that supports enterprise and personal growth as applied to the engineering work environment. We need to heighten the general enthusiasm for change as applied to productivity and workspace op-timism. All of us who are still active in the field need to seek out re-sources and experts that can help us readjust to the game so we can progress rather than just eke out survival while we address the new professional chapters in our lives.

Luckily for employers, employees, and consumers, resilience can be learned. This book introduces the specific steps organizations can take in order to train resilience. Resilience training focusing on four areas, (emotional, cognitive and mental, physical, and spiritual resili-ence) can improve individual adaptability and emotional durability. It can enhance an employee's attitude, quality of life, and decrease stress and anxiety by teaching a means of viewing life's inevitable challenges as opportunities rather than overwhelming obstacles. It can also infuse a workforce with a sense of agency and value that profits all members of the system.

As a result of the current global pandemic and reliance on established system protocols and definitions that have hampered necessary change, social and, as a result, economic systems have finally arrived at a moment of inevitable consequences (more are set to come). Es-tablished systemic constructs have resulted in a devastating cultural and financial ability to sustain and survive change, and thus, we have finally come to a "moment of reckoning. The *This isn't working at all...maybe there is another way"* moment. This present moment may be dark but learning from the generalized failure to prepare for the inevitable (some say catastrophic disruptions) leads to an incredible opportunity to make effective changes. We can train new modes of success. We can reevaluate how we run our businesses and modify the way we train people to produce more socially intelligent and adaptive societies.

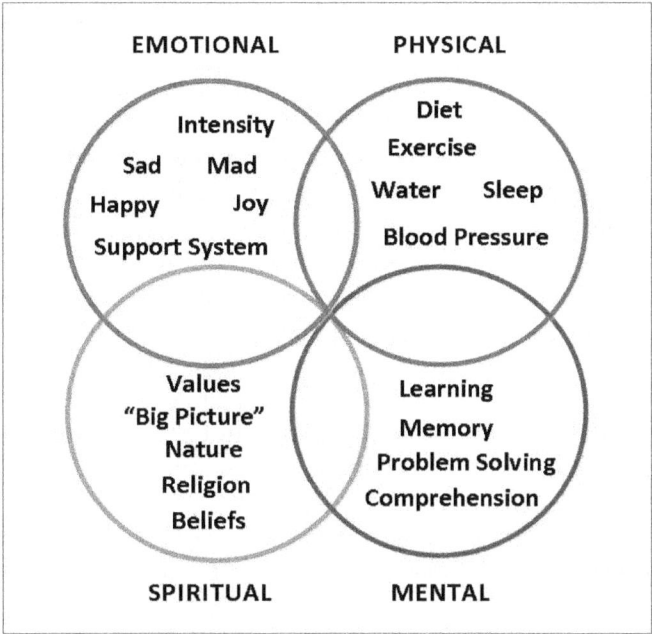

Figure 1

Stakeholders invested in all aspects of business are becoming open to alternative paradigms of interactions. They need new ways through new times and must consider approaches they would not have tried before.

There was no need in the times when a global health emergency was either an old *dead* issue that had been addressed via technology and science or an issue that future generations would have to resolve.

The arrival of the Coronavirus has created disruption, but it has also created a moment when change is essential. Often these moments can energize participants and make them better learners. Covid-19 and its iterations are here to stay. "It does seem likely that, under a wide range of parameter values, Covid-19 will continue to circulate as a seasonal wintertime virus" (harvard.edu, April 2022) [In fact,]... it might be necessary to have several years of intermittent social distancing to fully introduce the entire human population to the Covid-19 virus without overwhelming the health care system."

Embracing Change

Suppose we embrace the changes and use them as pivot points for future endeavors by facing facts and making sacrifices in the way we conduct business and in the way we create a community of productive units and employees. In that case, we can shift with the tide and not simply be overwhelmed by it. If we accept what seems like radical alterations in the way we develop, innovate, buy, sell, produce, and distribute services and products and in the way we create and maintain the workforce that will fulfill the needs of these new ways of doing business, we can move forward successfully. However, we must embrace a profound shift in value systems.

Currently, the U.S. corporate and industrial culture appear loyal to two strategies in adapting to disrupters in this instance, in reaction to Covid-19, but Covid-19 is only one of the powerful environmental forces pushing at us. Our first reaction seems to ignore long-term shifts and attempt to force a return to work, pretending that if we simply reestablish the: status quo" of going to work, everything else will fall back in line.

Unfortunately, the structures that left society without the resources to continue business as usual will not be enough to get us through to the other side with determination alone to overcome changes by ignoring them. The other standard option is to rail against the situation but make no meaningful change. As a society, we have come to rely on reacting rather than adapting when we try to solve problems. We want to typify problems and solutions as elements in a black and white grid and let our decision- making process be guided by the overriding systemic assumption that "if you stay aligned within the "good" category vs. the "bad" ones, then there is no need to alter one's world view."

None of these solutions will serve well in the long term; both are shaped by fear which prevents true innovation and shifts in behavioral patterns. Addressing the new reality in a novel fashion offers solutions and can infuse a working population with energy and promote optimism and innovation. The compounding crises of the 2020s provide us all a chance to deploy meaningful changes we should have been addressing already. We have known that a breakdown was coming for a long time but have failed to create the redundancies necessary to survive. This is a moment when societal evolution and adaptation are not optional. Now that the moment is here, we must embrace adaptive approaches that address the crises productively, not defensively.

Generational Resources

Resiliency will be a key to achieving these possibilities. At the fore are a millennial population raised in anxious times shaped by a sense of impending failure. They see a culture run with such a narrow sense of success that the issue of diminishing returns is the rule rather than the exception. This population is primed to be open to engaging in proactive modes of coping with unpredictable disrupters presented as a series of learned behaviors. Adaptive resilience offers possibilities so that one could take charge of the changes rather than wait to be rolled over by them. As for the older workers, the idea that there is a method of transformation that incorporates them can create more of a bond between the young and the old than we have seen previously.

It is possible to train individuals and groups to work confidently within the constructs of helping them acquire a comfort level with the constriction (and conflict) currently missing in much of today's workforce. The first step is to introduce the work population to the idea that systems are simply fluxing social constructs resulting from the interaction between cultural perspectives and objectives and the reality on the other. Armed with these perceptions, employees can develop a sense of agency and community and thus provide a more productive environment and a more successful one. They will feel ready to devise successful resolution strategies rather than resent and hide from them (Gallo, 2021).

Resiliency encompasses the desire to thrive by leveraging an adaptive mindset. With it, we can create new avenues of success with a community component. This effort requires the celebration of individual input that can aid in the disruption of a system because contraction is a means of healing and expansion. Suppose the reaction to disruption is a thorough examination of systemic and individual working structures at profound levels. In that case, the results can be radical evolution and emergence into a new growth phase as more effective entities. If we assume disruption is a constant, it must be addressed as a novel rather than a destructive force. With this force, the engineering workforce is headed towards the new growth stages and could do it with optimism. To promote and train creativity, agency, optimism, and a sense of success that is not based on supporting existing structures, organizations need to encourage a professional sense of comfort with uncertainty.

Training to become Resilient Engineers

Resilience training is organized so it can be codified to a certain extent while also being flexible enough to adapt to the changing needs of participants. It also includes the critical intellectual and emotional components that help participants master novelty. It relies on a certain amount of workshopping to tailor the skill set to the specific group's needs. As it is targeted as applied to the work activities rather than individual life skills, building tailoring to particular enterprises, organizations, programs, or even product lines may be necessary.

Unlike other emotional development or behavior therapeutics programs, our resiliency workshops foster engineers' development and communications and focus on workspace needs. These supportive skills include understanding the workforce's various behavior and emotional components and how their other functions make up a whole. We concentrate on teaching understanding and communicating via different abilities, skills, and needs amongst the individuals to create an adaptive and continually developing system.

Changing Values and Gaps: Culture, Climate & Tribes

Corporate Culture vs. Tribal Culture

In the previous chapter, we introduced the idea that groups with shared values and experiences organize as tribes. In this chapter, we further explore this concept. Corporate culture, corporate climate, and tribe values describe how the organization's values and behaviors are disseminated and interpreted by the individual and group elements of the organization: the workers. We use the terms "corporate and corporation" here to mean the organization. However, it also refers to a military branch or the military as a whole, another governmental organization, or an actual corporation. The terms have been incorporated into Enterprise Architecture and Business Development literature thus.

Corporate Culture, climate, and tribes are the social and organizational blocks that define and drive desired behaviors from the people that make up the corporation. These are the social drivers for workforce behavior, which in turn is what creates the unique products or services of the organization.

Cultures traditionally have been studied by anthropologists and sociologists who sought to identify groups and behaviors for understanding or control. In the 1970s, this area of study (Pettigrew, 1979) focused on businesses from a management or organizational focus. In this chapter, we discuss them as found by an outsider such as myself, a consultant and sub-contractor to many large corporate and governmental entities.

Corporate culture can change depending upon the goals of the CEO or other top management of the organization. The corporate culture emphasizes the critical attributes that the corporation values (Harvard Business Review, 2021). These are typically aligned with the kind of corporate structure it is

Corporate culture directs, impacts, and shapes the way we behave. It is composed of underlying assumptions and unwritten rules that often arise from the driving force of the organization (a president, chief, or head or board) and other individuals in a standard business environment. Exposure to new learning, different environments, and new demands may change these unwritten rules. To understand how this element can be captured in an Enterprise Architecture to help guide transformation within the enterprise, see Rao, Reedy, and Bellman's Certified Enterprise Architecture All-in-One Exam Guide 2019.

The corporate culture that has shifted and changed over time in response to outside stimulus is now experiencing multiple conflicting pressures with the desire to continue working with the formula that always worked while adapting to new circumstances and new workforce and consumer values. We concur with the previously mentioned Enterprise Architects, and numerous studies of cultures that the basic cultural assumptions underlying the corporation should be captured as models supporting the enterprise architecture; however, they are more often captured through memos, directives, policies, and handbooks given to employees.

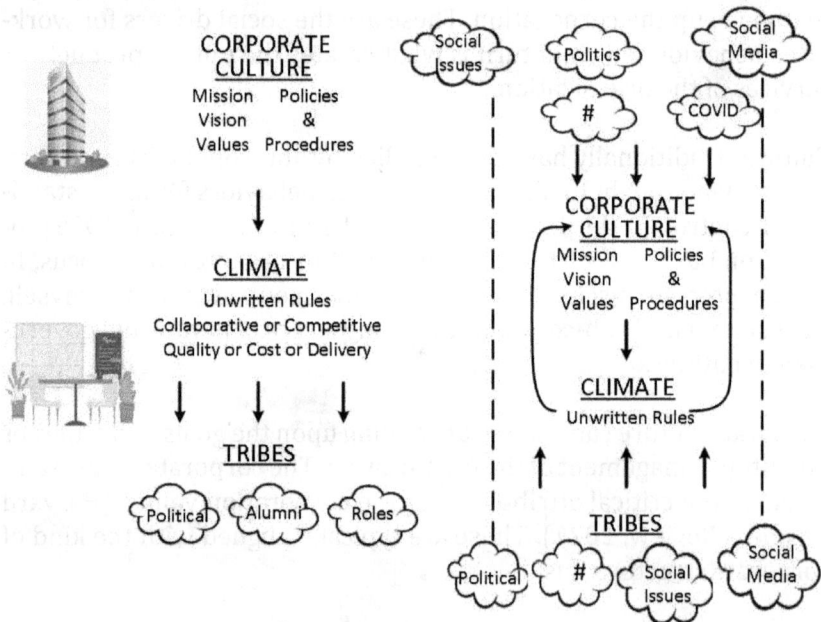

Figure 2

The cultural assumptions also direct the ranking of corporate strategies and inform leadership. Being shaped by underlying unwritten rules, how do we understand what we are to do? How do we know what it is to be an engineer in the United States, as an athlete at the Olympics, an immigrant worker in the United States, or a consultant in a new organization? We perceive written and unwritten clues that help guide us to understand a culture.

As a consultant in a new (to me) enterprise, I attempt to understand or break down my expected behavior by asking questions and observing. Is this an organization that values time in the seat? Are people rushing to be seen at their desks? Or is innovation key? Are other engineers introducing new ideas at meetings? I will often run across some negative assumptions "not invented here" means it's no good. Complicated is bad/good. Will I overreach if I suggest a working group or meeting to attempt to exceed the minimum requirements? Are there even written requirements? Perhaps this is an unconstrained cultural environment that resents written requirements to guide their task? We have worked with constraint and certainty in other organizations and would never work outside a written procedure or beyond a stated requirement. When asking how things are done and what the goals and values for a program are, I will often be introduced to myths, the executive who never gave an inch and forced the customer to buy what they were selling, or conversely, the organization that increased its quality standards during a program to dazzle the customer into expecting less. Tales of success and failure give me a good idea of how the workers are expected to behave and what behaviors are rewarded or punished. These are driven by a certain level of corporate culture (culture is often described as a shell game or onion layers that can be peeled back to reveal new layers).

In addition to the social cues and hints about culture, there are artifacts such as the handbooks, policies, training, and even office layouts (open concept to encourage sharing of information, locked doors, and protected discussions to support individual development and valuable individual intellectual property development).

I will then attach meaning to my observations of punishment and reward, other workers' concerns, and written or stated policies and practices. I also observe the meaning that others attach to these events and to the value system they observe. This then is the corporate climate, the meaning that we attach to the cultural artifacts (manuals, handbooks, memos training), and our observations. There are often issues that seem critical to the employees on the ground of the corporation that creates a misunderstanding of the corporate culture through the climate. One easy example is the location that the consultant is given. In some corporate cultures, production is valued over all else, there is a fairly level playing field, and everyone gets a desk to support their work. In many others, the location and amenities of the office are assigned to indicate the value of the worker and obtaining more amenities as a result of value is part of the corporate climate of that organization. If I am given a large or well-located office in these organizations, I am important, and staff will come to see who the important person is. In other places, all workers have similar cubbies or office spots, and there's no importance to the location of my desk or if I am even given a desk or have to float. I get clues to the culture when the first question is where your desk vs. what are you here for or what is your role or experience.

Once I have established my work environment and attempted to understand and analyze the corporate culture and climate, I then seek others with whom I can share some type of understanding. These people will help me further refine my notions of the climate and culture and help me obtain approval and resources. This is a natural process, not a defined business strategy. We call these groups tribes.

In any working enterprise, there are tribes and groups of up to 20-100 employees who share similar interpersonal characteristics and values, such as but not limited to political affiliation, social activities, gender, race, and/or role. Tribes may be observed as cliques, but they are different from cliques because these tribes can sabotage initiatives.

Historically corporate culture drove the corporate climate. Tribes developed within the organization naturally. Several of us observed around 2010 increased social pressure for corporate culture to comply with social norms. External societal culture began to drive the corporate culture. Through government mandates, these changes happened faster than ever before. Corporate culture had trouble catching up with the changes. Organization leadership was reprimanded and penalized for behaviors that were once rewarded without being offered training in terms of how to change and access the rewards once expected for behaviors that are no longer considered productive.

At the same time, more tribes with new agendas were entering the workforce; instead of learning and complying with the corporate climate, they sought to use their bargaining pressure as a tribe to change corporate culture. They wanted a more politically correct, family-friendly life culture. And in a case of shifting social-economic protocols, the tribes now influence the corporate climate so much that we have seen corporate culture turned upside down. The tribes are defining the climate and culture rather than complying with it. As a result, tribes' values and influence on the corporate climate have led to revolutions such as the "me too" era turning sexism on its head and the Great Resignation during the Covid-19 pandemic that started in 2020.

Now that the corporations and individuals have survived the pandemic shutdown measures, there is more cry for corporate change to accommodate worker values. Evidence of this are refusals to spend the time commuting, and resignations if required to work full time; this was noted in the Wall Street Journal and other business journals (Borchers, 2022). Many of the engineering workforce continued to go to work throughout the pandemic. The refusal of new workers to comply in the same way is confusing to the former group. There seem to be new tribes forming those that now push management to allow flexible from-home work and those that still call for in-office working and regular hours in order to coordinate the development and ensure productivity and quality.

The initial cultural stance of the corporation may not matter when the workforce refuses to comply, and more compliant workers cannot be found. Workers respond with concerns about the cost of living near work or commuting and the impact of this on their personal life. They refuse to bend their needs to accommodate the culture of the workplace. The new workstyle will necessarily be a blend of remote and local. The challenge in entering is that one must have access to colleagues and to hardware and software that are not remotely distributed. The other challenge is how to compensate those that must spend the extra time and money commuting in order to perform their work, something that was previously considered a part of the sacrifice made to obtain a "good job."

Currently, these profound changes in the corporate culture, climate, and tribe structure are playing out not only as a driver to change corporate culture but also resulting in gaps in product performance, quality, accuracy, and demonstrated discord between workforce groups. To address these issues in the new climate, we must turn to communications, behavioral inventories, emotional maturity, and other tools that help the human workforce components to share their needs and behaviors to strive for common goals.

Typically, we would start with an inventory and attempted understanding of the current corporate culture and climate. Although tribal units do not self identify and are not easily "inventoried" the divergent roles, functions, needs, and demands can be identified. With the help of a workshop and modeling tools, the tribal elements can be drawn out. This is done in order to forge a map for the future of the enterprise and the workers that can meet some of the demands of the workers and restore some of the productivity and quality sought by the corporation. In future chapters, we will discuss the behavior inventories and communications systems as well as the role of architectural modeling in building the workforce.

Throughout this book, we discuss the demographics of the workforce in terms of American generations using their popular names: Baby Boomer, Generation X, Millennials, Generation Y, and Generation Z. Prior to the Baby Boomers, the generation known as the Silent Generation, the last of this group was born in 1954 and are at least 77 years of age as of the writing of this book. A few of them are still found in the workplace, and their work ethics and values continue to exert pressure on corporate values and culture. We do not assert that all people behave according to their generational paradigms; however, the economic, social, and educational eras that each grew up in to help to shape a worldview. We are attempting to find common ground within diverging views, and so we generalize to attempt to find patterns within our human systems. The table below illustrates the birth periods of each generation, their common name, and their population, which will help forge a better understanding of the makeup of our workforce over time.

16

Generations in the Workforce				
		De-grees	Percentage of Workforce 2021	Numbers in millions
Greatest Generation	1928 and earlier			1.33
Silent Generation	1928-1945		2%	21.78
Baby Boomers	1946-1964	25%	25%	70.68
Generation X	1965-1980	29%	33%	64.95
Generation-Y /Millennials	1981-1996	40%	35%	72.26
Generation Z	1997-	TBD	5%	67.06

Fry, R. (2021, May 28). Pew Research Center) & Published by Statista Research Department, & 10, S. (2021, September 10)

Figure 3

3

Grief and Anxiety in the Workforce

Changing Interpersonal Expectations

Most of us feel that we are in an unpredictable and rapidly changing time, which leads to social, economic, and technological challenging days. The USA corporations and workforce seem to be at a tipping point, socially and morally, and economically. As individuals and employees, we feel that we are teetering on the edge, holding on to what is known while being battered by the changes that encourage us to let go. We continue to try to return to our previously rewarded plans and behaviors course without realizing this is a strategy. Sheltering as to survive Covid-19 heightened a common, profound sense of isolation. Many individuals are now unemployed, by choice or due to events beyond their control. Many job hunters: highly qualified job applicants, specialists, and skilled workers cannot find work. On the other hand, many jobs are going unfilled, leading to a lack of production and supplies. Some fear death or illness if they continue to go to work, while others crave the social, mental, and financial support found in their office environments.

Engineers and most mature members of the workforce believed they were in a phase of life when they would be able to slow down. Now they are discovering that they need to gear up and find new jobs in new fields of endeavor or accept a degraded standard of living. They need to reinvent themselves to move forward, and the idea is unsettling. They need to let go of the learned skills and behaviors that served those in the workforce for many years, which is frustrating and frightening. These workforce members find that their current coping strategies lack a good way to process and acknowledge the loss and uncertainty they feel in light of the situation.

The Rise of Social Media the Fall of Mentors and Colleagues

For all of us who had been actively working, it was a sudden change lacking structure to work from home. Hiding out in our homes, we sought community by peering at the world through the lenses of a variety of social networks. YouTube, Facebook, Twitter, Instagram, you name it, they brought community and social contract, but they distort things, and we feel a sort of guilt for using them. The accepted new outlets: radio, papers, and magazines, also became compromised, trying to give bite-sized stories and firm facts in a complicated and shifting period where no one trusted the information presented about the current diseases and our world's future. Many of us have become personally involved in fights over whether fact, story, and P.O.V. are "true" or right. If you spend 15 minutes on any social network, you will push away from your laptop more anxious and confused than before you logged on. Political events such as the siege of the capital, presidential elections, and even local elections enter the mix and become personal tragedies. The rise of reality television and the confused but pervasive perception that television stories are "history in the making" can override common sense and experience.

It is easier to have some other power dictate what to feel and think than to continuously filter through the noise of agendas and social media intentions to find the root of a story or platform and then formulate an opinion. This leads to division and polarity; instead of sharing ideas and forming understandings. We take shelter under a political platform, a social agenda, and religious belief and stop trying to analyze what comes to us; even analytical engineers are overwhelmed and seek an outside source of authority. It is not easy to bend moral compasses and values to match new situations and ensure that we have the right viewpoint. It is easier to jump on board and agree with what these outlets tell us regarding what everyone feels and knows.

If one uses social media to state or explore a position, the naysayers and "common man" commenters will quickly drown out any unique thoughts or doubts. This situation leads to doubt and confusion. What are my values? What was the situation? What is really happening? What is fact, fiction, and what is the made for media "reality". Am I a terrible person for thinking differently than the others? Beset by the need to rapidly find a proactive position without knowing exactly how to find sources we trust, we are dazed, confused, anxious, and overwhelmed.

The same complicated issues of truth, values, and beliefs confounded by media noise, spill over into the organizations that employ the workforce. The usual flow down of corporate culture that once informed workforce behaviors had already been questioned and compromised. Do we question the corporate direction and social and moral values or comply with their order to get things done? Which act will be rewarded by positive responses, continued employment, and successful program performance? Will the general population applaud our commitment to creating new products or punish us for working for "big corp" or making things that serve the wrong demographic? Will we be penalized for following old cultural norms discredited by the new social-pressures to be "woke," "green," and engendering?

Staying Connected

While we attempt to build immunity and resilience to Covid-19 and its mutations, we must also respond to the cascade of connected losses that change our communities. To adapt to these changes efficiently and successfully, we need to recognize our emotional and spiritual health needs. We must acknowledge and address a growing gap in communications, not just in how we speak and what we read and write, but in how we convey underlying paradigms and values that make up the platform of our daily functions and beliefs.

For the previous decades, engineers put work responsibilities first. We might sacrifice our feelings and needs to get back to work; we often would miss social and family events. We also found social support from others with shared values. Work also distracted us from grief and fear for a while and allowed us to feel productive and connected by participating within the workforce community. As children, Generation X members were known as the "latch key kids" because their parents worked, so they had to let themselves in at home. These children learned to be self-reliant and independent. They learned how to cook and entertain themselves at a young age but felt a lack of parental involvement in their lives. Many Generation X members have internalized the importance of being a productive employee. They saw that success in the workplace was more important to their parents than family together time.

When joining some of our working sessions, several engineers identified themselves as Generation Xers, caught in the middle. They learned to work hard and sacrifice personal and family time, but now as they reached the reward phase where they expected to be paid more and sacrifice less, they question the sacrifices they made for their careers. They are told they should have valued family and share more and work less. And they now seem to be expected to pick up the slack for those who now value personal time over job responsibilities. They wonder why the younger generation of workers is not required to step in and pick up the slack. They wonder what they can do to get the respect and seniority they deserve and to stop having to overwork. They are upset; some of them practically cry or shout when asked about this issue in group sessions. However, when asked if they are upset, they answer, "No, we just need to make the millennials work hard enough, to work as hard as we did." This group is feeling burned out. Many of our contemporaries are leaving their careers to find jobs at which they can function on a healthier level or are contemplating early retirement. Many are suffering from physical and mental illnesses. However, they seem unable to identify that they are feeling grief for a lost way of life. They find their unfulfilled expectations, experienced at what should be the pinnacle of their careers, disheartening.

Michael was wading through a damaging divorce. He came to work, but his performance was poor, and his behavior was disruptive. In trying to ignore what was an overwhelming personal disaster, he refused to ease up on his professional duties, which wore him down even further; still, he refused to discuss his divorce with anyone, which he needed to do. His behavior was partly shaped by the general historical feeling that personal issues should take a back seat to job responsibilities. Michael understood the priorities that had worked for him so far that were failing him now, but what could he do? There are a variety of responses to grief. Death, divorce, illness, and bankruptcy are only a few of the ordinary tragedies that afflict and affect a workforce on a regular basis. Add to those pressures the effects of sheltering and economic uncertainty in which the sense of anxiety and loss seems to be a continuing event, and people can feel driven to their worse behaviors.

One of the results of unemployment and sheltering has been a notable rise in domestic violence, even within healthy social networks (Engler, 2021). Private melodramas affect productivity and the general emotional health of the workforce and therefore affect the longevity, energy, and innovational capacity of organizational and enterprise success. Why are these situations rising when we are all home to-gether? Many people wished to telework before the pandemic but were told it would not work, as it would rupture the sense of commu-nity and the productive power of a team working together at an office or workplace.

Reducing Risks but Staying Connected

Remote working directives were intelligent ways to protect the workforce from spreading disease and were utilized to keep busi-nesses running. The switch may have saved people from increased disease spread, but it has also increased employees' sense of loneli-ness and eroded the emotional cohesion formed by teamwork. In the engineering environment, teams work closely together on programs and projects. In the service of shared goals, they also give up personal time and comfort for these goals. Other group members reinforce this behavior. Another effect of this type of team working is that concerns, issues, and risks can be quickly raised with easier access to the au-thorities who need to know. As workers increasingly become dis-tanced from each other and are often tasked to multiple projects with no clear chain of management, the ability to raise concerns and de-termine their criticality has eroded.

Keeping an Eye on Program Risks during Heightened Personal Risk

When laboring in the workplace, social groups form which offer a means of ethically checking personal behaviors; it is one of the posi-tive aspects of conformity. Due to teleworking, when we experienced a rapid change in moral and ethical practices, we also faced a loss of connection to supportive social groups. The result, combined with changes in communication methods and the team working environ-ment, has created serious risks in an inability to communicate. At the start of my career, I witnessed a mentor who had realized the danger in the design of an aircraft, running out to the tarmac to stop a test aircraft from taking off. Today we wouldn't know where the aircraft was or whom we needed to warn, and many employees would never have recognized the issue as something to address personally.

Teamwork

Moral and psychological normalities are essential elements of team-work. Employees fearful of economic loss feel an intense pressure to perform. People become confused and feel pressured by external and internal media sources when there are no physically present social groups and social interactions to check the messages against. The group of colleagues and supervisors who motivate staff and supervisors and help workforce members see themselves as part of the bigger picture are no longer close at hand and available for casual interactions. No one walks past the boss's office to the water cooler to have a word. Now it's an intentional text or call. This seems disruptive and might imply that we are not productive and that it's not an organic process.

Feeling part of a group work situation is a critical aspect of resiliency. Regular losses: divorce, disease, and bankruptcy are easier to withstand if one has an external compass that leads one back to normal but with teleworking, the group support that creates that rebound is lost. Gone are clear indicators of what is essential, including rapid ways of being rewarded for resolving problematic issues. Instead, we experience an endless list of "go back's," "call again's," and "resends" that encourage a loss of direction and motivation. The isolated working conditions mixed with the widespread fears of the pandemic and the fear of a financial free fall have enhanced the awareness of our fragility as individuals and in groups and ups the stress level. As value systems evolve, because of changing times, we are also experiencing heightened anxiety because the boundaries between business and personal arenas seem unclear, and we become afraid of losing total control of the boundaries between business and personal parts of our lives.

Change is a natural part of existence, and every successful enterprise is constantly adapting. But it takes time to become comfortable with change, and adaptation is always accompanied by at least shadows of resistance, sadness, and anger as the behaviors and protocols by which many workforce employees have lived all their working lives become outdated.

Diversity is another area of rapid change. We are told to celebrate it and embrace it. There are significant benefits to a diverse workforce, innovation brings an infusion of new points of view, but diversity enforcement can be a disruptive factor as well. In California, businesses must now register the diversity rates of their senior management and are fined if they are not diverse enough. We've moved from attempting to look for the most qualified or connected applicant to looking for the one that promotes the perception of diversity. What are the consequences? One is the fact that workforce members internalize the message that the color of skin or choice of gender is more important than productivity. The intention was to allow others to break the cycle of poverty and lack of opportunity, but the shortcut reduces productivity to support the optics. Either way, intelligence, skill, and ability seem less critical than presentation. This drive for diversity, while a good thing, can alter personal and professional expectations in a disruptive fashion as different groups of people bring alternate value systems into the workplace. To thrive and promote emotional health and cohesiveness in the workplace, organizations need to develop strategies that exploit the positive aspects of diversity while at the same time acknowledging and addressing the problems it poses.

We have lost track of what "professional" looks like. It is a relief that it no longer must look like a dark-suited white male, but it shouldn't look like someone dressed in their underwear talking to their cats instead of their colleagues. "Form follows function" was the old claim; the new one is that form is everything.

Generational issues (and their role in diversity initiatives) can create problems between coworkers. "Sharing" is the new buzzword, but you cannot ask employees who have been trained to keep their personal issues private to suddenly share some of those problems without training them and giving them guidelines. Every adult knows and can handle the fact that the workday will include disappointments. Long-term employees have a history of shunting these feelings aside or considering them part of "doing business" as they apply themselves to their work, but the feelings exist. They are a normal part of each day.

Employees of large companies are encouraged to think of themselves as part of a family or team. Contractors are often brought in to enhance the skill sets of this team and provide a different view of the workspace. Traditionally when hired, they hope to contribute. If they can help bring a project in early, even better, but once they succeed,

24

they are no longer needed and are expected to leave. Successful individuals being brought in are mined for their expertise and experience and then are let go, and this causes a sense of grief and loss. However, they may not acknowledge it out of habit and due to a sense of professionalism.

Changes in the workforce are very fluid, but the newer generations of workers don't work as old-timers expect them to (as the old-timers were expected to). Yet, they are rewarded for partially participating (in the eyes of long-term employees). Long-term employees who prioritize work over home life because that's what was expected are not being rewarded now for remaining true to these protocols. When older employees see younger workers being rewarded despite being late for work and failing to do their jobs (which would never have been acceptable in other times), they feel resentful. They feel diminished. They've been loyal to a pattern of behavior that was supposed to be rewarded and are now discovering that it is no longer the gold standard.

Technology and certification requirements are changing quickly, creating barriers to entry and change in terms of workforce opportunities. Those who have been learning new software when required and adapting their overall expertise and approach to new products and techniques suddenly find themselves pigeonholed into their current positions. Hoping for new opportunities, experienced workers in technical fields take the time to gain certificates and degrees in data science to enhance their existing skill sets. They then are told that their background does not count towards their subsequent placement. Others spend years building systems and learning the complex approaches needed for legacy programs, such as SaaS, only to be told they do not have the latest statistical software experience as they are passed over for promotion. Time was invested in training legacy workers on the newest software in the past. Newer team members applied their expertise to utilize the new programs. But for both populations, the reality now is that you may be sun-setted with the software without a certificate in the latest and greatest. Experienced workers, used to the notion that their products must be robust, are comfortable with a slower development cycle than those who believe that the newest shiny object is the winner and who further believe that it is more critical to stir consumer's interest (a user who also no longer expects full functionality and robust performance) than to avoid creating a product that does not fully function, The goal of trying to keep the spotlight by constantly changing software capabilities rather than functionality, creates yet another area of change and stress. Should we concentrate on making the best Access ™ database to serve our clients, or should we spend our workday learning the newest SQL programming so we will not be left behind?

There are many fields where trained, highly educated, and successful professionals achieve critical short-term success only to be laid off once they meet immediate organizational goals. Without the ability to transition, they are professionally stalled. But transitional strategies are not intuitive; they need to be taught. Suppose you are an instructor in a university or community college. In that case, you are likely an adjunct with a Ph.D. or a Master's degree trapped in a job that will never provide job security or promotions or pensions, no matter how dedicated you are to your tasks and no matter how many degrees you have that you got because of a promise of secure well-paid work at the end of the trail. Stay in these jobs long enough, and you become obsolete no matter how well you keep up with new educational goals. Because of the pandemic, hospitals are hiring more nurses but only daily. Asked to commit at some personal risk to a job that needs doing, these educated professionals who also paid for their training will likely be released from service once this extraordinary time passes. Like many professionals with a specific skill set, the nurses and the instructors will not be rewarded with long-term promotions and will be laid off once they are no longer needed. Most people accept that change is a constant, but adapting to changes is not as intuitive a process as we tend to think. "What are the rules?" and "How do I advance?" are questions we now need to address in a new work environment.

Sharing

Personal sharing of stories and feelings is complicated. Sharing personal information was once considered unprofessional exposure. Now it is a required or desired behavior. Employees are expected to share with the group so that they may become "part of the family" at work, but where do we draw the line?

But you cannot simply insist on employees who have learned to protect intellectual propriety and defend new development from theft.

Some groups and individuals question this need to share (or refuse to consider it), while others consider it an essential aspect of their work environment.

It is always assumed that there are benefits to the new protocols, but that does not mean it's easy to adopt them. Arthur, a technician, was hired for his technical skills, not for his ability to interact with others. He relies on his strengths in technical writing and editing to succeed. He put his head down and took vacation time to learn new software and editing methods to update the skills for which he was hired. He tried to establish himself as an expert in software ready to help the newcomers, only to find himself written up for sharing inappropriately or not sharing enough. There seemed to be some mysterious new standards he does not understand that have suddenly become critical to his continued success at work. So now he's confused and resentful. Dan, a fellow programmer, is also told to start sharing. Like Arthur, Dan has spent the better part of his professional life keeping personal matters private, not ever sharing his private life at work as it had been deemed inappropriate. Without the skill set to know when, how, and what to share, he starts accosting people in the office with personal information. During a group sharing/team building event, he describes a significant personal history event that occurred during his army service, but this is deemed inappropriate by the group leader who reprimands him. Eventually, he suffers mental and physical ailments from the stress this brings. In another group sharing exercise, Julie shares that she feels frustrated that people who lack the necessary technical skill sets are being promoted while those with the most vital skills are left behind.

She is one of the skilled and feels unappreciated and overburdened with the responsibility of making up for the deficiencies of others. After sharing this concern, she is informed that she does not demonstrate appropriate interpersonal skills and is later written up for not sharing her distress at the loss of her pet. You cannot effect change without providing instruction, and failure to do so degrades the degree of emotional health that sharing is meant to promote. Learning the art of appropriate sharing as a form of team bonding is no different from learning a new software package; neither one should be assumed to be known.

Younger workers often embrace interpersonal bonding and sharing. Older workers see younger generation workers rewarded for freely showing their feelings. Then they are reprimanded or ostracized for not doing the same; they conclude that hiding their grief as part of professionalism was a wasted effort. They start to feel that the sacrifices they were expected to make are no longer rewarded, and the professional behaviors they painfully learned are no longer appreciated. Seeing a younger generation being rewarded for what seems to be unprofessional behavior is confusing. Not knowing how to compete according to the new rules is downright angering.

In addition to new rules on sharing, there are gender norms that are also changing. In currently or previously male-dominated industries, women used to be told to keep personal stuff out of the workplace. This expectation has also changed with the newer generations. It is okay even encouraged to express grief and anxiety at work.

Is the change a good idea? Does it help workers better concentrate or feel more supported? It may, but most organizations have a whole generation of workers who don't naturally acknowledge or express intimate feelings at work. This situation causes them feelings of loss and grief, sometimes expressed as frustration and anger. People need to learn how to express emotions appropriately they were never before supposed to discuss and then need time for it to become a habit. There is a sense among older workers that younger workers feel more entitled to their grief and are super sensitive to what they define as emotional abuse. This may or may not be the case, but you cannot create teammates and co-workers without new strategies for navigating these different points of view. Instead, you have tribes on the floor who resent one another and do not know how to communicate with one another.

"I don't know what I can say."

Political Correctness

Navigating through the shoals of political correctness increases the emotional load on the workforce. Intended to encourage tolerance and respect and promote diversity, this new imperative to be fair and unprejudiced has made people overly concerned with how they express themselves. What are the suitable subjects to broach, what are the right words to use when you do, and when do you use them? What common saying or learned habits might be offensive? How do you assist staff and supervisors when personal issues affect office productivity without asking the wrong question?

Bill, the owner of a plumbing company, hires a bookkeeper. A week later, she comes to work dressed in pregnancy clothing. She had not mentioned her pregnancy during her interview, and now Bill is concerned about family leave and needs to know if he should hire someone to take her position if she needs the time off. They could not have a dialogue about this topic during the interview unless she brought it up, and he cannot now ask her if she is pregnant. So now, how does Bill open that dialogue regarding personal matters without being offensive?

"When I was mentored, this was how you dressed. Now what?"

In the past, many women were required to dress a certain way. They were expected to wear high heels, dresses that were not too short, and blouses and business suits that looked like men's shirts and suits. Women have spent a long time learning these rules but those rules and putting together these wardrobes. Now, these rules are changed; there is more latitude now in terms of how they may dress but less clear guidance. Demonstrating personality in the way one dresses is now celebrated. On the hand, great. On the other, *"Have I just wasted all this time trying to fit into a size and shape of a businesswoman because now it works against me?"* Women used to be required to do "better than a man" to overcome accent, clothing, and race to succeed. They were still passed over because they were women, not because of their skillsets. Now, these survivors face competition from diverse kinds of women walking in the door who use the fact that they don't fit in as their selling point, ahead of their skillsets, which often as not, are not comparable to women already in the program.

Angela, an African-American, a single mother getting her Master's in Organizational Development, is still uncertain if her efforts are worthwhile. There are niches for her because companies now seek diversity, but these same organizations are not promoting women, especially black women, in the workforce. They don't offer mentoring or coaching to help these women succeed once hired. On the company side, many executives are at a loss as to how to address the new initiatives that are precipitously dropped in their laps. If they don't mentor, it could be because they don't know how and are uncertain about the standards they are supposed to meet, in part. After all, the standards are vague, and they keep changing. We don't train transitions well. If the new reality is that employees need to be ready to move on once they have achieved specific goals or complete certain tasks, why aren't we training that adaptation?

Training Adaptation

We grieve. We are angry. We are anxious and unable to negotiate our way successfully as much as we try in the professional arena. There is a point to be made by individuals who played by the rules they were taught and who today cannot seem to compete with a younger unskilled diverse group of individuals who come to the work floor with different ideas of responsibility.

The good news is that people are naturally resilient. Grief is a commonality everyone understands and has experienced. Recovery is a natural process and a healthy response to loss. How fast it occurs and how much give and take and attention is needed to help members of your workforce through loss varies. However, effective general protocols can be implemented to facilitate resilience as it impacts individuals and the workforce group. "Most people deal with grief reasonably well. We get through it. We are pretty resilient," Dr. Bonnano, professor of clinical psychology at Columbia University, who has studied grief and epidemics, says. He also notes that grief is painful, ubiquitous, and adaptive (Bonanno, 2021).

Grief is transient. According to individual coping needs, when most people grieve or experience anxiety or deep uncertainty, they move in and out of darker and lighter phases of the experience. It is possible to address diverse workforce needs with generalized protocols that can be easily adapted. It is possible to develop the personal tools and protocols to equip all workforce stakeholders for survival, adaptation, and progress. Instead of retreat and despair, it is possible to train recovery in the face of personal losses, economic disaster, pandemics, long-term grief, and anxiety. Before you can move on to recovery, you have to acknowledge the suffering driving you. Feel it, see it, give it a name, and only then can you apply strategies and coping tools to help you and your teams move forward.

Paying attention to changes that need to be made is key, even if some of the changes can seem discomforting. It is possible to maintain focus on the long view in terms of organizational productivity and creativity while triaging to meet crises and stabilize organizations that themselves are entities in flux, particularly during this time when the crises are open-ended and likely to require several phases of reformation as the society, we live in embraces meeting new possibilities which are as unknown as the troubles that feel as if they are simply destabilizing catalysts.

Practical Steps to Recovery

Engaging employees in authentic purpose will benefit the organization in terms of the workforce on a group and individual level. It can also encourage client loyalty. The client-supplier relationship is buffered when resilience is promoted, and clients are businessmen too. They are suffering from the same issues; therefore, to see one company successfully move their workforce into resiliency provides clues to other organizations that might still be struggling. We can teach one another to be ready to recognize, respond, recover and thrive in the end, even if what success looks like is unclear for the moment.

Be transparent about what you know needs to be faced and what needs to change. Be empathetic and frame the realities of seeing those experiencing difficulties with anxiety and grief as possibilities for positive change without diminishing feelings or forcing individuals to process their issues faster than they can.

Create and become aligned with a clearly designed sense of purpose which can contain numerous "I don't knows" and "this could change tomorrow if the information changes" and still foster a sense that current uncertainties and crises can and will result in innovation that will bring the whole crowd along on the journey.

For example, the American people have watched their federal and state governments fail to educate and equip their citizens to effectively cope during this global pandemic. In part, this is because the scope of the problem and how its existence spun off into other problems so quickly hampered the government's ability to cope. This reality, in turn, created a considerable amount of public distrust so that when viable protocols were proffered as solutions, whether or not to follow them became a socially divisive issue. Those government officials, globally and nationally, who were transparently clear about what they knew, about what no one yet knew, what they/we were doing, and how they/we needed to change how they/we managed during these series of crises by in large succeeded because they brought the population along with them on the process of triaging discovery. Informed individuals feel empowered. Those officials who hid what they knew and did not know and offered scatter shot, uniformed solutions lost vital support and created a stasis of anxiety that stops people from feeling supported, supportive or trusting.

You also need supervisors who can model what they teach, communicate, train, and create for resiliency to work. In this way, you can encourage the vital trust that defends against employee turnover and failure, which in turn can promote innovation and success in these uncertain times.

4

The Value of Organizational Resiliency in the Workforce

Thus far, this book has concentrated on how to develop and support resiliency for individuals within the workforce. At a higher level, the workforce is part of an organization that may be a company, division, product line, governmental entity, etc. These organizations are either a part of or the entirety of the enterprise, whose purpose is to create products or services. An organization can be seen as an entity. Although, it is comprised of groups and resources rather than solely connected individuals. For the sake of this discussion, it is acknowledged that individuals still drive organizational success. However, we can also consider the organization's behavior as a whole just as we do that of the individual.

Organizations that focus on damage control and getting "back to normal" by using only the business and process models that were in place before the pandemic will find it challenging to address shifts in market demands, supply chains, and labor shortages. They may lack the structures needed to provide enticing benefits to retain and attract workers (CNBC, 2022, "Big Jobs Growth"). They cannot grasp or exploit the change in labor and consumer concerns that have accelerated in the past few years of rapid changes.

Organizational resiliency relies on perceiving and predicting market forces and acting to benefit from changes, including climate, social, market, technology, and political forces. The inherent capabilities and structure of an organization are supported by flexible thinking and the approaches of the various individuals that drive it. These are challenged in the post-Covid shutdown world. Supply chains have been altered. Consumer buying power and demands will continue to change rapidly. The social revolution that shapes organizations has been on the move for some time now, and it has solidified. Individuals demanding the organization comply with their social and moral systems are triumphing and forcing a power shift that must be normalized within business practices. Today, employees require increased telework, less focus on co-located or centrally located offices, and more flexible schedules. In addition, the time spent isolated has added impediments to connecting, working together, and creating cohort understanding. This means that organizations' means of working and creation must change and become more flexible to encompass the new workforce demands. The good news is that this is the same flexibility that traditionally has been used to make new products/services or derivatives or to move into a new market domain.

None of the pressures affecting the workplace now are new, but they resonate powerfully in this Covid Age. The rise in resignations, retirements, the ghosting of jobs in response to pressure, burnout and unemployment, and activated furloughs in the previous years highlight a sense of helplessness and lack of organizational control of the workforce and acceptance by the organization of its responsibility to support its workforce (BenefitsPro, 2022).

In response to the eroding element of highly productive workers, many companies are issuing upbeat public notices claiming that together they (and their employees) are bucking up and meeting the new changes enthusiastically and with success. "Welcome Back!" "The Worst is Behind Us!." "It's a new day, and we are moving forward!" kind of notices add to the pressure. They imply that it would be best to ignore the fact that everyone is in a new state of uncertainty. However, because of rapid changes and adaptation needed to meet the demands of the new remote, social distancing existence, a significant number of the workforce population is running on empty (Parker, 2022). Many are not certain that they possess enough native resilience to endure until the state of the world changes for the better or settles down (Kochar and Bennet, 2021). It's difficult or impossible to build a forward-looking plan when the future is unknown, and this situation is problematic for engineering personalities that require facts, models, and projections to build upon to adapt. Simply stating that we will return to normal when things are not normal and then utilizing former processes built to satisfy different paradigms leads to concern, confusion, and hopelessness.

"I am now only doing the exact amount asked of me"

There seems to be no reason to try to build the big picture. There's no reason to run issues "up the flagpole" or note concerns if one is no longer rewarded for meeting goals and making sacrifices. Losing the detail-oriented nature of the engineering role and abandoning the big picture thinking undermines any organization's ability to produce high quality products. Many major engineering companies already see this erosion in quality and performance. It erodes the quality of life of the consumers and producers within organizations and in the larger communities dependent upon their products.

It is posited that we are at a pivot point in terms of the existent business climate. Some businesses are adapting and even thriving because of the turmoil and the changes thrust upon them. Restaurants are experimenting with a wide variety of take-out and delivery options. Some successfully increase their margins as they learn how to manage new online, in-home, delivery type demand (McKinsey, 2022).

Small farmers who lost income when restaurants and supermarkets stopped calling are now directly selling to homebound customers. Due to multiple shifts-shifts in the environment, government support, workforce availability, and lost products, customers are now more willing to experiment with new brands, new solutions, and new ways of purchasing instead of just relying on standard outlets and products. In response, the old favorite corporations are forced to reposition and alter brand purpose.

Corporate powerhouses such as Unilever and Proctor & Gamble have started prioritizing supplying household cleaning products over skincare products as the demand for the latter has fallen (Gallo, 2021). This shape-shifting strategy needs to be applied to all successful organizations. Instead of changing, enterprises are attempting to return to an outdated concept of typical damaging their potential in employee productivity. Many intend to continue to "run the maze" they have developed over time, hoping that returning to previous behaviors will eventually result in expected rewards. However, costly best practices and processes that once resulted in returns on the initial investment were built for different paradigms and are now obsolete modes of behavior.

By refusing to acknowledge that the workforce is another aspect of production and an enterprise asset that must be reassessed and redeveloped, entities cheat themselves of the potential to re-energize employee purpose and ambition. Those organizations that encourage emotional resilience by designating workforce members' potential as part of the solution (instead of categorizing them as a cost) in their bid to return to normal will benefit from the pivot point once things start to improve.

Managing Groups in Recovery

Organizations must foster resiliency in their approach to workforce development: hiring, working locations, schedules, and communications. Corporate culture and climate must become more fluid to support the individuals within the organization, offering them the control and power to reduce the uncertainty, feelings of futility, and lack of reward. The big picture thinking that brought production and innovation to high levels in the 60s and 70s needs to be fostered and rewarded.

Many supervisors recognize the cost of strained interactions in their workforce but do not know how to apply a fix. They do not have the training yet. Luckily this early failure to exploit an opportunity that can be fixed. Traditionally, the managerial inclination is to punish those who do not perform as expected. Unfortunately, in the diminished workforce environment with the "cancel culture" and "great resignation" simply leaves the organization with a reduced capacity due to a lack of employees. The successful, more resilient approach is to identify the new skillsets (capabilities) needed to enhance development. Organizations need to utilize those individuals with the developed survival skills and encourage them to embrace the opportunity to share their knowledge and their experiences with those who need training in this area, which would create a bonding opportunity. Then organizations need to identify and support good communication by building a new platform for understanding and providing the opportunity to learn about different means of communication and learning.

We are not necessarily saying that everyone needs to be friends. However, it is possible to create a supportive community effort on the work floor where teambuilding occurs that will combat the clique building sense of divisiveness that drains resiliency from everyone (and every enterprise). When older employees and younger employees react differently to the need to learn new protocols, there needs to be a way to create bridges instead of rifts.

For example, in the medical field, a hospital needs more nurses on the floor but cannot find regular staff to hire, and they are addressing a short-term need that does not match the long-term budget. In response, HR resolves to shift from full hires to per diem, which in some cases suits newer, younger staff members who treasure flexibility above certainty. They also begin hiring traveling nurses for a month or a quarter at a time, paying their housing and travel costs. The new nurses enjoy the freedom to choose to work and to get to travel but want the same respect as contracted employees. Long-term nurses feel insecure and put upon when they are expected to show temporary nurses the ropes in addition to attending to their duties, and they feel underpaid. The temporary nurses feel resentment when required to take on so much bureaucracy and learning for a short-term position where they are "essential." Long-term staff feel unappreciated and that after mentoring new staff, they will be back to doing everything without extra appreciation when these short-term folks leave. Resentment between the two groups grows as a result.

What if the two groups could be trained to see a picture in which different kinds of responsibilities could be meted out in a way that is strengthened by the two types of hiring categories? What will it take to get the traditional workers to understand that the new nurses can bring more contemporary skills and energy to the job so that it is worth the time to "show the ropes"? What if the two groups could be trained to view one another as part of an alliance that makes the new changes work? Multiple dialogs need to take place for this to happen.

There has been much burnout of existing staff in some public health and nursing arenas during the COVID surges. Many today are welcoming new training in communications and resiliency. They see a need to learn how to adapt and thrive in a high-pressure, constantly changing workplace, and the offer of these workshops from their organization has enticed many to stay longer at jobs they were about to leave. They are learning about the different types of people with varying ways of communicating and different needs. Thus "long term" folks see the benefit of the training and gain new skills paid for by their organization which is a form of support that boosts employee morale.

Employees also learn different ways of classifying individuals, from the Meyers-Briggs assessments to the Wiley Disc training; many of the formerly underappreciated systems for building understanding and categorizing behaviors are now providing a helping hand to bridge the gaps in understanding and values.

Is Your Organization Ready To Pivot?

Some organizations do not have the tools to change yet, (because of physical, capital, and social limitations). These organizations' structures, missions, and visions dictate whether they can benefit from changes (or design critical changes that need to be implemented). Some entities, such as capital-intensive long timeline industries, may not survive. Will coal mining come to an end? What about nuclear energy production? What will happen to the monster truck building? Will all the airlines survive the pandemic shutdowns and continue to support their customers, or will there be downsizing, mergers, acquisitions, and bankruptcies that end their existence as we know them? Many organizations are currently in perilous positions (travel agents, catering companies, U.S.-based extractives industries, and entertainment enterprises may vanish from the landscape). There is an inescapable level of uncertainty facing us now about whether Covid cases continue to rise or fall. Further, the traditional mentor-mentee method of sharing corporate knowledge seems to have failed.

More middle-aged and older employees are considering retirement, resulting in organizations losing valuable legacy. This trend accelerated during the current crisis but was already a significant source of corporate knowledge loss. The boomer generation often retired without passing their knowledge on, and now Generation x is following suit, with many taking early retirement due to job stress. With little or no mentoring processes in place or placed in name, they also take their expertise with them. The newer employees do not value the information thinking it can all be found on the internet and YouTube. A quick correction needs to be made before all this knowledge is lost. There are tools ranging from those same video services to internal web-based knowledge banks made by a few organizations. We have spent time creating a systems model-based knowledge bank for several organizations to provide future resources and direction. The interesting thing is that the process of interviewing and recording the older employees is often enough to make them feel empowered and interested in continuing their work.

It is essential to capture this knowledge before it is gone; we've worked with companies who overlooked this and are abandoning product lines or spending millions reverse-engineering them. The outgoing employees expressed that they were undervalued; both lifestyle and salary options declined. They noticed newer, less experienced employees being paid more and doing less, so they left. They had created the required products, but there was little documentation of their processes and none of their workflow and decision-making process. The tools exist to capture all of this, but the most crucial part is for the organization to place a value on the data capture process. Younger employees can gain experience and knowledge when led through the interview and modeling processes. Create a draft information model and road map, then interview key personnel who contributed to the current product line, ask what they do, how they do it, how they make decisions, and what they document. Try to capture the processes and practices from their heads and get them on paper. This, in turn, can lead to an information model-based web interface to store knowledge. It can be utilized to script tools to support the workflow.

This process requires that the organization place a value on the knowledge capture; it will generally be considered overhead rather than a billable or applied project. Then the resources need to be committed; the experienced employees need to be compensated and rewarded for this work by paying them, interviewing them, and showing that their work is valuable.

Another essential part of this process is promoting communication between the different generational groups. To capture the knowledge, the organization can offer its newest workers guidance on how to interview and discuss information—a first formative step in bridging the communication gap.

At this time, formal communications training may also be helpful. In our practice, what is most valuable is finding ways to define behavior types and communications processes as are found in applied MBTI or DiSC. Utilizing the systems and enterprise engineering process of defining information flows and querying to create complete requirements are additional tools in communications bridge-building and knowledge capture. The final steps are to script modern tools, big data, knowledge management, and OO databases to support the knowledge capture process.

Organizational governing bodies must utilize knowledge management and expanded benefits and enhanced salaries to retain older workers with a depth of experience and attract new workers with energy at the start of their work life cycle. The resilient organization must adapt new tools to transfer knowledge and values from one group to another. The old assumptions of shared values and behaviors no longer hold. The gap in worker behavior and values comes when the workflow is being pressured to change due to the current economic climate.

An organization with a resiliency strategy in place can spread the idea of resilient protocols across a broad group of individuals no matter what the differences are and create a progressive unity. Because this kind of organization already has a comprehensive view of the different value systems at work on the work floor and has experience introducing new system designs to its organization; it can learn to use its older workforce to implement the necessary adaptive strategies.

Enterprise Architecture and Recovery

It is not possible to have 20/20 vision. It is impossible to be endlessly flexible. Any organization that endures must identify (and communicate) its strengths and weaknesses, in sum, its capabilities, to serve future demands. Enterprise Architecture, already a familiar process, can be valuable in this instance; it can provide initial tools to identify the mission, vision, capabilities, and services that shape successful organizations. It can be used to reshape communication modes and essential enterprise capabilities that allow an organization to change direction, identify new capabilities, and enable the workforce to support evolving goals as they are reshaped to meet new needs.

Most organizations govern and change in a top-down manner. The organization is made up of experienced leaders who have learned to balance the needs of customers, shareholders, investors, or voters and those of the end-users of their product. Using traditional elements of corporate climate such as notices, brown bag meetings, bulletin boards, and corporate wide memos, they guide the workforce to desired behaviors, or they did until recently. It was assumed that the workers would wish to comply with these directives to gain rewards, keep their jobs, and climb the corporate ladder. Little thought was given to helping individuals learn how they are expected to behave or how the individual workers required the corporate leaders to act. To have a resilient and adaptable organization, we have to foster communication of these needs in both directions; from the individual worker level to the corporate leader, the worker demands become a part of the corporate balancing act. Indeed, there have always been demands for fair pay and decent working conditions. However, current demands are more complicated and require a significant shift in thinking to encompass gender identity, work life balance changes, emotional maturity support, and flexible working strategies.

For the last decade, in the Enterprise Architecture and Systems Engineering community within the aerospace and defense industry, there has been a focus on building emergent enterprises, resilient systems, and adaptive systems. The traditional focus has been on developing the enterprise's products, namely resiliency, and adaptivity, by utilizing awareness of the shape-shifting tendencies of a healthy, dynamic process that drives productivity and innovation. These emergent enterprises support the development of adaptive systems in which gains are achieved by defining system boundaries and system values (without over-constraining the solution space) until new technology can be plugged into the existing overall systems. Emergent enterprises naturally foster changes that quickly align with evolving value systems. Individuals, groups, and the environment will often present novel solutions as they evolve. Emergent enterprises can also immediately recognize the value of new-borne systems and novel solutions and quickly put them to work. Already there are models and approaches in existence designed to create emergent enterprises developed in service of getting better and newer technology rapidly fielded that benefit from new ideas and solutions.

A ship, for example, can have a last-minute propulsion change, and a computer can accept different hard drives; it is not all defined at the low level. This reality has forced more thinking about the intended effect of a system, how changes affect it, and how the capabilities and constraints of a system play into strategy and design. The intention is to reverse the trend to over define to prevent failure. Over-constraining too early in the design feels like a safe bet, but in reality, this retards a product's efficacy. In one example of the cost of this kind of planning, the model and manufacturer of the tires of a particular vehicle were proscribed before it had been determined whether the said vehicle would land on wheels or where it was supposed to be capable of landing. This flawed idealism prevented emergent design and thinking processes from fully exploring the item's potential (or the criteria needed to decide its potential). Could it land on the skids? Should it land on floats? Will it land on water, sand? etc.

Enterprises learn from mistakes but regularly become too rigid and disastrously constrained. It now appears that we are in a period of constraint as many new engineers find it difficult to think about designing a new system within a new environment and instead tend to think of iterative improvements in existing systems (new apps, bug fixes, a combustion style engine running on a battery vs a completely different vehicle, UAVs with cockpits). Emergent and adaptive drives are attempts to free some of the collective intellectual power to build new and better systems that more easily adapt to needs and demands and available technology and thus can solve problems without expensive and destructive rigidity, but that also maintain lessons that are learned in terms of constraints. In an emergent system design, a navy aircraft constrained to land on an aircraft carrier that must be serviced by existing equipment and supported with existing skills and parts could be imagined in more than one possible shape and size and be driven by more than one kind of possible propulsion system.

Another strong drive, in terms of design and planning, has been aligned with Agile design protocols. Initially intended to help develop software elements with less formality quickly, Agile design began as a way to develop code within a defined system space, relying on unnecessary formal requirements, development milestones, and waterfall processes. It was managed by a small, tight-knit group that had a clear set of goals and was expected and allowed to use their experience and innovation to develop what was needed. This protocol has been more broadly embraced for the development of both software and hardware to counteract excessively slow controls and development processes and to allow more rapid technology changes. It results in more misses and failures, but development happens quickly at a lower cost.

Similar approaches are needed in terms of redesigning the engine (the workforce) of many enterprises. The workforce (a.k.a. people) are essential elements of any design, development, production, and sale of systems. Work only within defined processes and practices, and we succumb to the temptation to define these components too narrowly and thus fail to achieve our goals. If we decide that employees must be in their office seats at 9 a.m. to be productive, the result can be an employee who feels that as long as they are in their seats on time, they are doing their job and entitled to pay. The sudden pandemic driven switch to telework shows that the "butt in seat count (one must be sitting in their office) is not the only way to ensure that people are working. Unfortunately, telework has not been as successfully productive as many enterprises require. However, now the workers don't want to give up their flexibility and saved time from commutes to return to the office. Thus, a blended approach with plenty of additivity and resiliency will be required. All telework at undefined hours does not work because workforce members need to interact to share ideas, issues, and other elements of work. The reality checks, work syncing, and idea sharing don't happen in remote work-from-home environments. The endless zoom and skype calls became a distraction rather than a way to co-work. Employees also need the social aspect of in-office type interaction, which feeds their personal needs and supports innovation and creativity. It also allows casual interaction that builds understanding and communication skills to replace this in the telework environment will require more than mandatory web calls.

The new workforce needs social and personal focus, social and environmental responsibility, gender identity freedom, and political transparency. These demands have been building over time but are becoming critical as we enter the post-pandemic economic recovery process. Resilient enterprises will adapt to some of these demands and will foster the ability of their workforce to adapt and change to support the new demands put upon it and develop the emotional maturity to accept the constantly changing normal of our new environment.

The good news is that crisis moments spur change and innovation. Alterations we need to make now because of urgent needs are now easier to accept, and people can become more willing to invest in new ways of interacting and problem solving. We can learn from disruptive moments in ways we can't when things work well. If we can successfully implement strategies, sell a plan that offers a way the group can work together and use one another's strengths and shore up one another's lack of resiliency to move forward and think about your values and goals and what is the definition of better?

5

The Whole Person Approach to Developing Overall Adaptability

Returning to Equilibrium

"For every action, there is an equal and opposite reaction" (NASA 2015). When pressure is applied one way it modifies other behaviors. We generally ask, "Do you want it fast or do you want it right?" Because we can either apply pressure to go faster or to do it perfectly but not both, there is a natural conservation of effort.

The best way to support resilience building for the individual worker is to incorporate all the aspects of individual adaptability into your training paradigm. However, the workforce development process must limit its reach in certain areas including the physical and incorporeal. There is room for improvement in how the organization supports the individual in these areas, but it cannot, by law as well as preference, direct individual development in these areas. However, it would be a mistake to avoid them. The whole person approach is essential. In Enterprise Architecture both internal and external elements are captured in the model, and this is the essence of the whole person approach, capturing and acknowledging the role of all four categories of personal development but not controlling them.

The whole person approach to developing overall adaptability relies upon building sustainable coping skills in four categories: mental (or cognitive), emotional, physical, and spiritual-incorporeal. The goal is to help individual workforce members gain the ability to recover equilibrium easily when faced with large and small (the large and small calamities). The whole person and systems approach makes it possible to define and train the skill sets and attitudes needed for this balancing act without getting "out of scope" by directing physical or incorporeal behaviors.

Change and Resiliency

Change is a constant. The human being is a creature living in constant flux. Therefore, maintaining a healthy state of resiliency is a never-ending process of continuous building and growing. The four areas to develop in terms of resiliency are also always in flux. We need to focus on one or another kind to varying degrees depending on situational requirements and because each person has a different combination of strengths and weaknesses. Some people are mentally more effective problem solvers, some are more emotionally robust, and such. These areas and their robustness will change throughout a lifetime, sometimes weekly, sometimes monthly, sometimes remaining stagnant for years because they remain workable as they are. Our capabilities, behaviors, and emotions also dictate how we communicate with each other and what face we present. Learning to understand how others communicate and learning how to speak to their strengths in reference to the workplace, is another capability that can and should be taught as a part of the resiliency building process.

The Value of the Half Empty Glass

One way to visualize the flexibility and toughness needed to recover and to appreciate how the process of maintaining equilibrium works is to think of a cup and its relationship to its contents. The cup represents stress, adversity, the changes they affect, and the limit to how much any one person can stand to take on. The liquid inside is a naturally evolving flow of energies. Once trapped in the cup, these energies are pressurized and stopped up. The water level in the cup rises in response to the way daily life stressors increase pressure forcing the water level upwards. Some of the tensions are the results of interactions with supervisors, co-workers, friends, antagonists, and family who pour into our cup. Whether they are successful or not, human interaction creates stress. We want those life affirming energies to remain free flowing. We don't want them trapped in the cup that we need because it is a necessary reservoir that allows us to set aside certain pressures as necessary. Sometimes the water level rises at a precipitous rate from a furiously flowing tap (the result of trauma) until it overflows. We want to keep our cup as empty as possible, draining the contents regularly and depressurizing the contents so that the cup does not overflow. We want to have a margin or buffer between the liquid and the top of the cup, so that when a large event, or crisis, occurs we can recover, adjust, or bounce back as easily and quickly as possible. Some people have larger cups that can hold more water, some have smaller cups, some cups are long and elegant, and some can be folded so that they fit into someone's pocket until they are needed. The different shapes, sizes, and kinds of cups are the results of a combination of genetics, environment, experience, and age. For the most part, we want to work with our cup to make it bigger. Sometimes, we may need to alter the shape, this is resiliency in a metaphorical sense. Some of the strategies we train will effect simple and small changes but strategies, just like the drops of water, (or stress) filling up the cup, can help maintain the water in the cup at a reasonable level.

Physical and Emotional Aspects

It can come as no surprise that the way we feel physically affects our emotional state. The way we care for our bodies can support or undermine our health and thus all areas of resilience. Our physical brain needs as much support to enhance our mental and intellectual abilities. Human beings are compelled to seek pleasure and avoid pain as efficiently as possible. This is a statement of human psychology that has been asserted over the millennium by a multitude of notables engaged in the examination of the human drive towards success commonly referred to as the Motivational Triad coined by Dr. Doug Lisle from Epicurius, to Jeremy Bentham to Dr. Aaron Beck (the "father of cognitive therapy") professionals who spent lifetimes studying human behavior and who left behind a massive body of work on the subject. But often this aspect of personality can entangle human beings in self-defeating behavior patterns that wear them out and keep them from reaching goals that in the long term will serve them better than the short-term ones they often pursue instead.

Think about the last time you tried to save money by cutting out some of the luxuries you allow yourself that can make the days flow or feel less stressful. You've decided to brown bag it to work, bring a thermos of coffee instead of stopping at Starbucks and take a walk when you need to destress instead of head down to the cafeteria or the local bakery or nearby fast-food facility. You shopped for the thermos, bought food to make lunches, and dumped a set of running shoes into your car so that you can take that walk. But by day three of all this rearranging, you found yourself missing not only the actual treats you'd allowed yourself previously but you realized the anticipatory aspect of knowing these goodies were going to be a part of the day was also making you feel stressed. Maybe not super stressed but de-

47

prived. So you ignore the brown bag, use the drive-through at Starbucks on the way to work, and instead of taking that peaceful stroll around the block stroll back to the local bakery to enjoy selecting, buying, and noshing on your favorite snack. Very quickly the long-term benefits you would have realized had you stuck to your original intention seemed as if they would take too long to achieve and require too much discomfort. You went with instant pleasure which you could achieve more efficiently and more quickly than waiting for the benefits that would have come in time had you been able to prioritize the value of delayed gratification over immediate pleasure. The trade-off was causing dissatisfaction and discomfort that you wanted to avoid and that you had to regularly confront before you realized a long-term economic benefit. But by understanding the motivations that drive you, you can adjust how you are implementing your change so that the adjustments are less discomforting. Maybe you could make smaller changes, allow for moments of small rewards, use a friend's assistance to motivate you, and ease some of the discomforts you wish to avoid. Maybe by being more acutely aware of small happy moments you won't give up would allow you to make changes and a commitment to buying patterns that would help you save money.

The Mental Aspect

The mental aspect of resiliency for the individual is hard to pin down. The way to change this aspect of personality can be likened to Colonel Boyd's OODA loop (Observe-Orient-Decide-Act), iterative, four-stage problem-solving model used for improving a process or carrying out change when you do not have a full dataset (R. 2021, "The OODA Loop"). In this case, the process is a mental protocol that drives behavior. You may be familiar with this at work from military training, continuous quality or process improvement efforts.

In sum, you experience discomfort or notice that some part of the process for addressing pressing problems is failing. It is a less logical aspect. You notice something in the system is off but cannot say what or possibly even why you know this to be true as the problem it will cause has not occurred. Nonetheless, you begin to anticipate what the problems to come might be and start to ask questions about the process examining it for weaknesses. Then the problem is revealed, and you arrive at the moment of providing solutions with some ideas already in hand that promote the success of actually resolving an issue.

You act on your intuition and intelligence and innovative capacities and shift into altering the system so that it shifts into a new normal which allows you to relax and get ready for the next set of problem-solving acts. The mental shifts can fail because it takes a new mindset to see failures as simply steps on the way to real solutions, but this framing of problems and solutions can also be trained in the personal arena in a way that makes individuals and enterprises resilient.

Human beings have a natural toughness that can be exploited to help us as individuals and as members of our families, communities, and workforce, to thrive in uncertain times. The saving pennies example is not an example of a dire emergency, but the difficulties entailed in achieving success in this area are comprised of the same conflicts between basic needs, fears, pressures, and self-confidence issues that are part of every personality evolving process.

We naturally respond to change by aggressively seeking solutions that allow us to change or continue on our present path to match the challenge. We may decide to wait out the problem or resist the change altogether. As you are reading this book, you will continue to use your mental and intellectual capabilities to take in new information and give it interpersonal context. This is natural. When faced with adversity or change, we respond personally to build a mental picture from our perspective. We evaluate how a change affects our environment. We assess what we can do to succeed, then we determine what we intend to do and investigate what we do not know in terms of resolving issues.

When thinking about what you are reading, you have both an intellectual and emotional response to the new material. The four categories of resilience are constantly interacting. Here the intellectual and the emotional parts of humanity are integral aspects of the successful learner. Our emotions support the intellectual process that generates the feelings that support our intellect. Furthermore, the way we feel and think can affect the quality of our resiliency and that of others as well. We can learn how to bolster control over both aspects of this feedback loop and thus enhance our and others' ability to adapt. Resiliency is both an individual and team sport.

The Incorporeal Aspect

Tending to the fourth area of focus, the incorporeal this is often considered to be the spiritual aspect. This is where humans understand what or who is most important to us and what guides our sense of purpose and moral values, it could be other individuals, community, nature or religion. It refers to our essence (spirit) in terms of our values, and our faith. By understanding the compelling why of this area, we can align our performance and engagement to what matters most to us and thus support the other three aspects of resiliency further.

As we dive deeper into our four areas of focus - mental, emotional, physical, and spiritual, and examine the strategies we can use to increase our capabilities in these areas, we will notice how work in one area can affect the other focus areas. Building resiliency is not a one-and-done affair, it is a process of continuous building and growing following that OODA loop process of observing the current situation orienting to changes, deciding what to do and choosing to act while observing the outcome.

6

Resistance and Constraints

We have thus far built in what aerospace engineers would call a blue sky scenario by assuming there are almost no constraints on re-engineering the enterprise and its workforce to pivot and adapt to change. We have identified culture clashes between generational tribes and considered what is needed to build a new corporate culture and climate that adapts to the rapidly changing values and realities in the current world of manufacturing and design. We have also examined and explained the resources of the individual workers who must be sustained so they can flex and pivot with the realities of any enterprise's novel challenges.

However, in the real world, we need to recognize old and new constraints to adapt to them and model to foster success. Limited financial, physical, mental, and incorporeal resources shape productive strategy. A small capital think tank cannot suddenly manufacture aircraft. An artist is incapable of writing code. Heavily capitalized energy industries such as coal mining and burning to electrical generating cannot change overnight. If all that was necessary to change development processes to make them in sync with shifting social and economic values were to foster the essential characteristics of a balanced worker and provide an understanding of the demographics of the workforce, perhaps you would not need this book. Organizations would not need workshops to help them develop their new enterprise models, capture communications and value systems, or learn communications and adaptation.

Understanding how to instigate change is essential to success. When change is pushed too fast, companies can collapse. The coal mines of the west shuttered, generating facilities closed, and whole factory towns were destroyed because the industries that created products and financial success could not adapt fast enough, and they simply couldn't. There are several parts to the resistance to change. The cost and speed at which you can rebuild are often finite factors. Legal constraints such as those that affect how workers are utilized and how land or property may be exploited often prevent organizations from adjusting protocols and thus can constrain how companies enact change. Costly permitting and certification systems capitalization and market forces can also delay expeditious changes. Governing individuals or boards resist change even when existing economic models they have relied on in the past fail them in the present. To say the least, it is often disconcerting to risk total failure by moving in a new direction.

Perhaps the most significant hurdle is the individual resistance to change. Engineers are arguably a demographic that is inherently resistant to accepting change, particularly in terms of amending processes and practice. They don't mind learning new engineering tools, but they often need clear direction, support, and proof that a change is warranted before they will accept this reality. Generally, this is a good trait for those developing critical and complex systems, but it can also restrict an organization's progress.

This resistance to change in high-tech and high-risk environments often confuses the outside observer. I have been called on this issue numerous times when I accept the risk in a design, plan, or recreational activity (such as rock climbing) but refuse to take on risks I find incalculable or related to rapid change, aspects that I cannot quantify. A high known risk is more acceptable than an unknown risk, which might be lower. People, particularly those who favor analytic and quantitative approaches, are often more comfortable repeating known patterns. Organizations benefit from following patterns they have "learned" and that have provided the highest quality results in the past. Lessons learned and best practices often result in fewer mistakes and higher positive outcomes. But sometimes, pursuing this policy is a severe mistake.

A symptom of this reticence is a workforce push-back. Gordon Graham, a 33-year law enforcement veteran, co-founder of Lexipol, a risk management expert, and a practicing attorney, presents a commonsense risk management approach to public safety professionals. He focuses on this issue when he discusses how devastating failures usually occur in the high risk, low frequency quadrant of events (Graham, 2020).

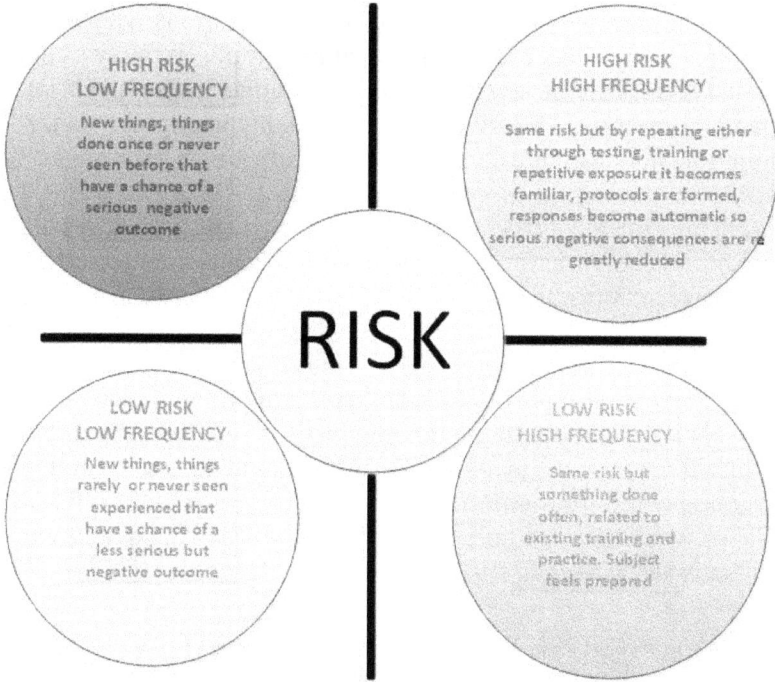

Figure 4

The careful processes we follow when designing and incrementally and deeply testing new high-risk products such as aircraft, nuclear systems, power plants, or medical equipment all seek "high frequency" for high-risk design changes. Through this process, enough is learned and practiced with the new system that deviations and failures become known, planned, and trained for.

This is how engineers prefer to modify behaviors. They like "high frequency" change, something well known and tested, framed in a low-risk event. Trying to create a new automated PowerPoint is a low-risk event. Trying to make a new autopilot for commercial aircraft is a high-risk event. When it comes to using computer-based tools, much of the engineering workforce resists change, preferring known software packages that have worked reliably versus newer systems with more bells and whistles, but which need meticulous evaluation and testing before they can be considered "known" and reliable.

We must adopt new behavioral patterns in situations where the environment and values have changed. For example, in today's culture, we must cope with the low frequency but intense "noise" of social media and fancy computing systems that virtually juxtapose reality and simulation, making it harder to identify genuine high-risk issues. This noise is an increasing threat to those critical elements of the engineering task protocols that might be subsumed and not addressed because of these distractions. In recent years, we have noticed that it is common for contracts and essential documents to get lost in newly structured Google drives. Deadlines are lost in the heat of structuring different project management tools. Combine these losses with the reality of constant Agile scrums, and suddenly the big picture is lost, and programs fail. Add to the mix the fact that while many engineers continued to work at the office during the Covid-19 stay-at-home period, some worked at home and still refuse to return to the office. New workers working from home often fail to do their jobs, and we see that "balls are getting dropped" as a consequence.

How do we now accommodate the health needs of the existing workforce and the dynamics required by the new emerging workers?

The first necessary and often overlooked step is determining the exact goals and priorities you intend to pursue. This seems like a simple step, but too often we take for granted values and goals that no longer apply to us or our situations and this choice hampers progress on a number of levels. The ability to accept big changes is critical, but when environmental factors change, we tend to address these changes without realizing that we also have to alter value systems as well in order to successfully meet new needs.

First, we need to identify necessary changes and relate them to pre-existing systems. If we are working from home, what adjustments do we need to make to address the loss of community and personal contact that aids progress? In the office, people do not spend all day on social media or cleaning their kitchen because the presence of others and office restrictions eradicate these distractions. The company of others, impromptu and planned meetings, and shared workspaces in the office help the group focus on the tasks, deadlines, and demands and keep individuals from inappropriately attending to social and personal needs, wants, and other pulls. If I am physically at work, then if a concern arises, I can immediately walk into another office, find the contact for a specific process or call an important meeting and thus can quickly identify a likely issue, raise concerns with others or instantly reassure myself that it is not a serious concern.

The initial attempts to work from home, like working in the office, involved (and still involve) endless web-based meetings. These were not as effective as in person experiences. Over time everyone fell into the habit of letting webinars run while doing other things, i.e., ordering online, responding to a Twitter feed.

Making Change Work

In order to trust the new environment and to embrace new value systems we need to learn them, internalize them and repeatedly test their components to make them feel familiar and trustworthy. It does not work to simply swap one experience or tool for another. If we are to substitute the couch for the office, Zoom or Skype for a morning meeting, we need some structure and process to increase our familiarity and trust in the new practices. We should test our online meeting tools, identify what workers are supposed to be doing from home and script interactions via webinar, phone, text, slack etc. to ensure that the new systems work to keep the workers connected and engaged.

We need to practice, model and rehearse how to communicate online so that messages are not lost, and that distinctions are still being made between business and personal issues, and between fact and opinion. We need to reestablish lines of communications in which real concerns can be raised and responded to expeditiously. The "frequency" of the daily work process needs to be re-established and re-learned. Working together in focused time periods helped organizations to support others that had to continue design and development during the "shutdown" period. These successful entities focused on returning to professionalism, limiting communications in web meetings to the task at hand and to creating new outlets for "water cooler" types of discussions.

This is how we make change more acceptable to the older engineers in the workforce and how we can make new policies and processes more known and comfortable. This is only one aspect of the change;

more senior engineers, for their part, also have to learn how to communicate with (Chapter 7) and understand younger workers who come from a more software interface based, complicated learning environment and who have a different set of values for work and work-life balance, a different approach to deadlines, criticality, and appreciation of risk. We begin by capturing their working systems and values, usually via discussion and workshops on how to blend these newer values with the older. The outcome must be incrementally tested and challenged and rehearsed to make forward progress possible.

Reaction not just Resistance

We also need to address outright reactionary behaviors. "The kids these days." "Not invented here." "It's all new tech." "It will never work," or "Why should I do it differently, this worked before." "Tried and true is better than new," or "You are too old to understand type dynamics." Or simply, "You could never understand." We tend to resist change and align our tribe against new ideas. Risk of failure causes resistance, and this resistance is healthy up to a point. We need to reduce the risk of severe consequences from doing something untried or unknown. But this reactionary aspect of human nature is often built on irrational prejudices rather than on rational analysis and it often prompts us to push away change when we need to embrace it.

The best approach to overcoming this resistance is developing communication and understanding with softer skill building. Bare reaction uses a different part of the brain than analysis; it is a "fast-twitch" type response. To many of us, it appears that the entire United States population is too busy reacting to think or perhaps too focused on minutia and noise to think well. It will be challenging, but we have to move the workforce back to a thinking mode to restore equilibrium and peace and focus on issues that can cause product failures vs. annoyances and dislikes that don't matter. We need to break down complicated systems, emotions, and behaviors into models and organized systems to create environments that allow individuals to calm down and see how they fit in and interact with the whole. Companies utilize business cycle, financial, economic, and enterprise models to do this; individuals within the workforce have to adopt these as well so they can stop reacting to every stimulus with attempts just to discredit or push away too much stimulation.

We were told Covid-19 would kill us so we had to stay home, now we're told we have to go back to work. Conflicting messages from a number of sources regarding protection and consequences, mix with political messaging. When faced with "return to work" direction or vaccine mandates the instinctual brain takes over as the thinking brain can't find a clear understanding. Our values and beliefs have shifted to support the reactionary position. We all know clearer messaging and transparency is needed. "I'm not going back to work" "It is not worth the risk," etc. Workers crave this from their organizations however they may still push back regardless.

Stimulus for Change

Workforce members are not the only ones who exhibit reactionary behaviors. The workforce is also part of the consumer base that continues to react instead of think. This is not a new Covid problem, it is an acceleration of an existing problem that has been pressurized by environmental and human rights concerns, Covid, supply chain issues, mixed messaging and social media pressures. Our world has gotten more complicated in the last 50 years. There are so many new interfaces to learn, disaster stories to read, big systems are failing, little systems are failing, value systems conflict news and social media make it all seem overwhelming, new and as if each aspect is the sign of an extinction level event. It seems as if disasters are coming one upon the next, climate change, crop failures, disease epidemics, moral failures of leaders and the demands that businesses suddenly change from captains of capitalism to leaders for social responsibility.

Suddenly organization boards must be composed of those with an ethnic-socio-economically diverse background, the State of California has mandated registration of the background diversity of company officers, seemingly making diversity rather than competence the highest employee value. At the same time the stakeholders are expected to bankroll those with less resources. Supply chains have changed. The treasured just-in-time supply system is suddenly devalued because it cannot guarantee the flow of products to the consumer.

In order to help workforce members adapt to these changes we must rely on the same framework, defined modeled changes to the system, evaluation and mitigation of impacts, training to make the new familiar and emphasis on communication systems. There will continue to be reactions for and against changes but in the work environment at least this can be broken into planned calculated changes to enable thinking and ration response.

Consumers and Change

We have discussed the shift from the corporate apex in which a governing board or individual shapes corporate culture that workers comply with to a structure in which worker tribes are now directing changes in the workplace culture. A similar shift is felt from consumers as they demand the corporate culture adopt more socially and environmentally responsible policies that also caused changes at work. Direction from management and early warnings regarding changes can reduce the workforce reaction.

The demand that the organizations become more socially responsible is complicated. Organizations are directed to quickly become more diverse, to pay fair wages, to recognize more gender identities and to become more ecologically "green" as well to accommodate work from home needs for health protection, accommodate multiple gender identities at work and provide social support for isolated workers.

This is best accomplished by identifying what changes can be made then relating them to the existing corporate climate and creating a roadmap for change to allow analysis, and input before the changes take place. Other changes related to limited workforce supply, supply chain issues and quality issues, also have to be absorbed so relief is needed via planning and road mapping of the controllable changes. Some changes must be balanced between behavior and physical, an example being the response to the demand for recognition and support of multiple gender identities.

Gender Identity: Support vs. Constraint

Many older facilities have only one bathroom on each floor, it is already a challenge to create men's and women's rooms, if others are to be accommodated, what can be done? Creating more bathrooms is extremely expensive and sometimes impossible. Having two sets of bathrooms already inconveniences those who have to go to another area or another floor for their bathroom. When faced with additional gender types and needs, do we alter workforce behavior so that some share with other gender types or do we build more bathrooms? Do we set up usage schedules? How do we cope with the inevitable "bashing" and "prejudice" will interfere with equilibrium and efficacy of the organizations community because of a lack of resources and personal space? In the future, buildings could be more accommodating but again there is a cost to adding plumbing and rooms set aside for biological functions rather than work which will require further communications to address the problems of diversity in the workplace.

Mission and Vision

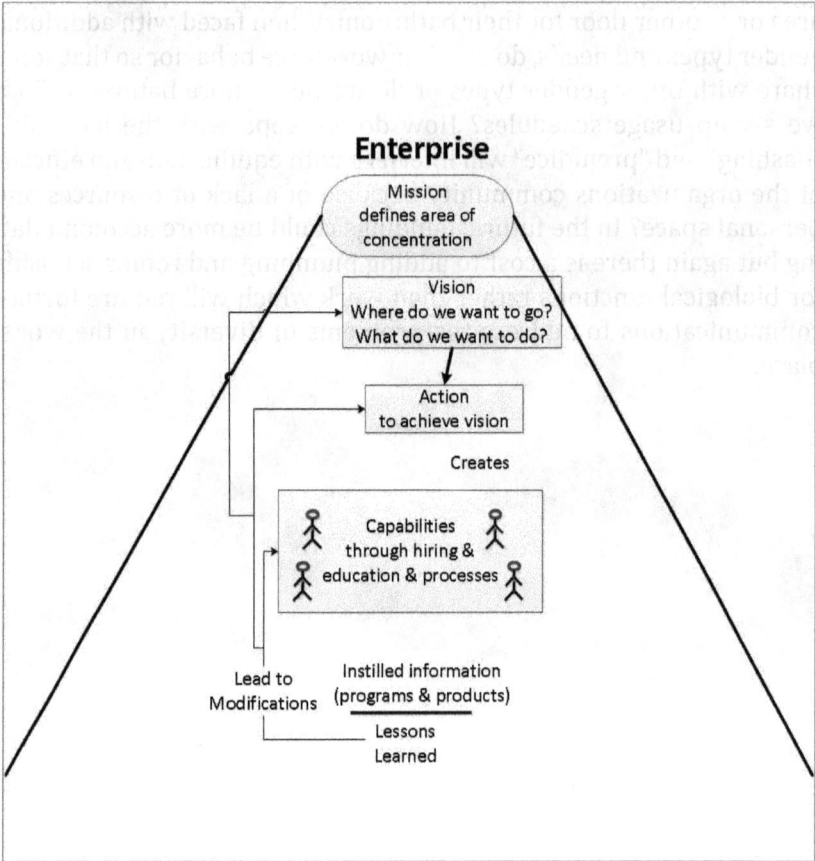

Figure 5

In figure 5, the mission and vision of the organization are illustrated driving down to capabilities. If transparency and communication are keys to reducing reactionism and can support analytic thought, then the organization must have a clearly defined mission and vision that forms its new corporate culture and climate and reinforces workers' values. To navigate through change there must be a clear vision defining the organization and its goals. These are fundamental concepts of Enterprise Architecture (EA) and are essential to even business or enterprise to guide its growth and development as well as to secure investments and funding and regulatory approval.

The mission of an enterprise is the focus and purpose of the organization. Governmental organizations have legally established missions that cannot change without legislation. Large established entities such as Amazon, Boeing or IBM have long term missions that serve their customer base however these could be altered under the extreme pressure of customer base shifts. Many business and Enterprise Architecture articles and books have been written that describe how to write a mission statement, explain why they are essential and how they must be integrated in primary EA models. We advocate reconsideration of and a rebroadcast of an organizational mission statement that will nominate the workforce as an essential component. This statement needs to describe how new changes relate to the mission and define the vision that motivates employees to continue to serve the mission and gives them agency in regards to integrating rapid change and development in service of the larger goals.

The vision of an organization state is often described as aspirational. Where are we going? What will the journey look like? This vision may be in flux as it must align with shifting external forces. This is an essential aspect of all business development but cannot be set and forgotten, this pivotal period of business history requires revisiting and carefully crafting and then communicating the external and internal vision for the company.

The company vision will be realized by shifting capabilities to support new projects; capability makeup and configurations will also change. For the workforce this means they can expect new hires, layoffs, and more education. If they are offered a roadmap that allows them to understand not only what is to come but that also empowers them, you might get more buy-in. Another area to address is the shifting rewards, as vision and value change so does the reward. "Loyal workers who have accumulated a lifetime of learning to comply with the company culture must still feel rewarded and empowered even as the culture begins to change.

7

Communication as the Interface between Workforce Components

In the previous chapter we defined capabilities as a part of the mission and vision flow (Figure 5). An organization's vision is realized through actions designed to achieve desired outcomes. The capabilities that support this outcome are acquired and developed to create the products and develop the programs that are an outcome of the organization's focus and development. Capabilities, in broad terms, are the ability to achieve the intended effect (Russell, 2004). To hone these capabilities, an organization needs to build and acquire and train: a workforce, skillsets for workers, tools, processes to utilize tools, and processes to achieve its vision.

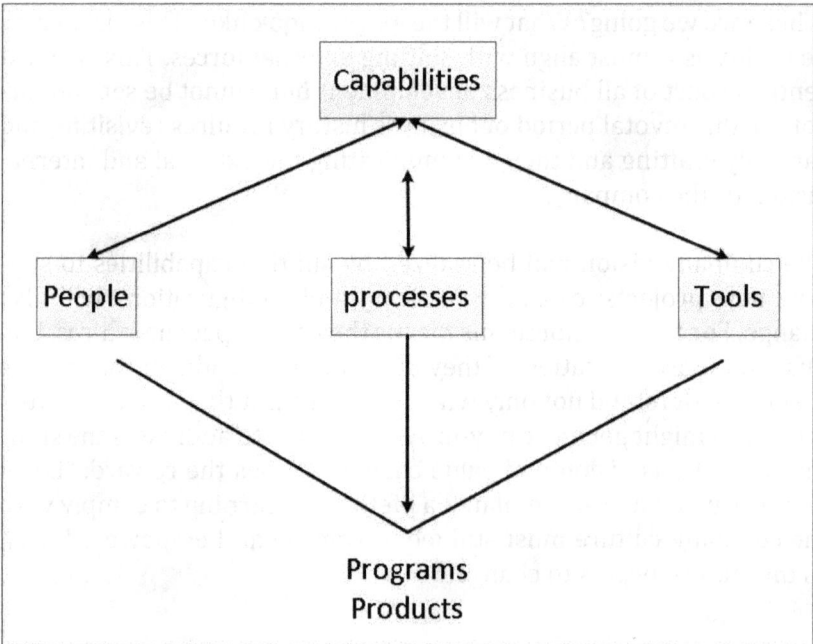

Capabilities

People   processes   Tools

Programs
Products

Figure 6

Tools including costly hardware and software (with high learning curves), change slowly. Processes can evolve a little quicker than capital purchases. However, they are built on the experience of previous outcomes, which are based on scientific and mathematical principles, legal constraints, and the quality and quantity needs of the company's products. Training and experience can modify workers' skills. This book concentrates on this final set. The skillsets usually promoted by companies are tool utilization and specialized practices. We have taught these applied skills for many years in a series of workshops: "How to Write a Good Requirements," "Intro to Enterprise Architecture Models for DoDAF," "Requirements for Combat Systems Engineering," and "Intro to DOORs ™, SLATE ™." These are applied or external toolsets. We offer workshops designed to develop more internal capabilities such as absorbing change, returning to equilibrium, and communicating across multiple personality or behavior types (Wiley's DiSC, applied Meyers Briggs, (MBTI). We have established that the missing skillsets in our engineering workforce are communications and internal resilience skills. These are different from the general life skills taught to make us better people or more balanced and are targeted to the engineering workforce. So, they become an element of the individual's capabilities. We would call it a component in our Systems Engineering models.

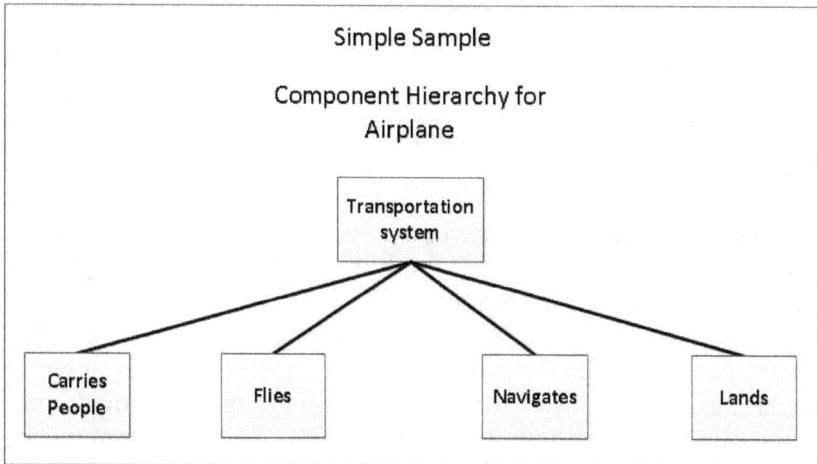

Figure 7

If we consider building an airplane, we begin by dividing the different parts of the aircraft into components and other hierarchies to allow us to collect requirements into systems that can be developed and tested. There is no one right way to do this. The systems engineer usually utilizes their experience and knowledge of both the program and the audience to create an initial hierarchy to collect requirements and input. The components describe the units being built and can be further broken down, usually resulting in specification and test documents. In the case of the program, more than one type of hierarchy is used, but in this case, we consider the components. We utilize this type of model to ensure we have captured everything necessary for product development. Does the aircraft need to land? Did we write requirements for that? Is take-off different? What else is missing? And the many other tools to test so that we know we are not missing anything in our understanding and development plans before we begin. It is also an excellent way to initialize dialog with the stakeholder to ensure this end-user has specified enough of the functions and behaviors of the system that can develop a complete system. Did we forget to specify that we want to navigate by instrument, carry other cargo, and so on.

As we further define the components of our system, we begin to also look at the interfaces between the components. Depending upon the system, we may have simple or complex interfaces that carry information from one area to another.

In terms of building an adaptive workforce and reducing emotional exhaustion from trying to lead or demonstrate to workers who have different values, we know that enhanced understanding supported by improved communications practices is essential. If we need to forge communication between more senior and younger employees, take the example of how to transmit information. The older workers valued learning from their mentors, but much of this paradigm has shifted for younger workers with new cultural norms. The demonstrations by the older workers are taken for granted (that group will do the heavy lifting and will overwork) and ignored by younger workers because of the new cultural climate; this group rejects overworking to corporate deadlines. If the older worker were to communicate and open a dialog rather than demonstrate, more could be learned, and compromises or pattern changes could be reached.

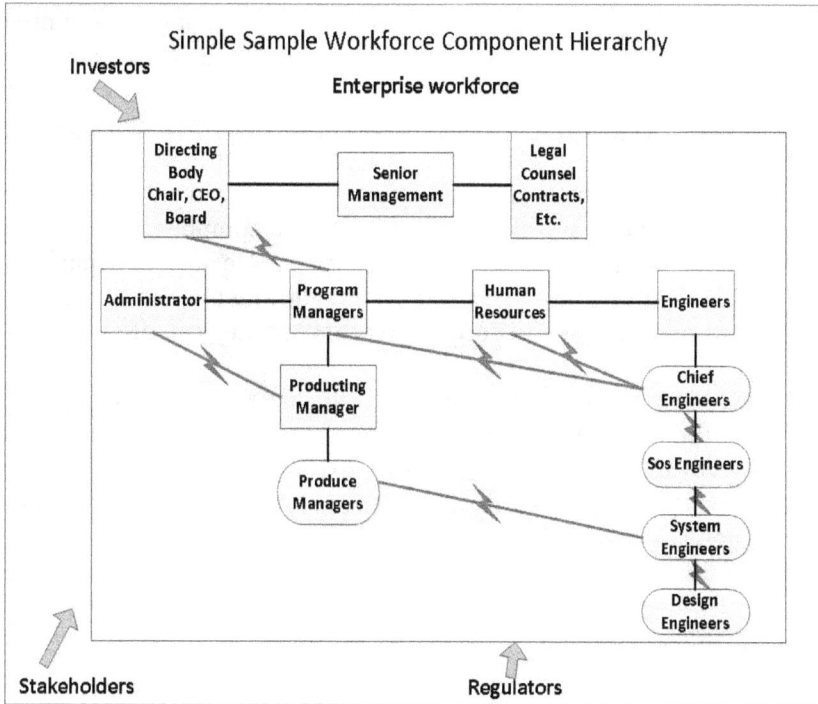

Figure 8

In figure 8, we consider a workforce components hierarchy. We have modeled some outside forces that drive behavior with arrows from investors, stakeholders, and regulators who influence the behavior of the enterprise workforce. Looking at the diagram, it seems evident that outside forces are being satisfied by the first tier of worker types, whose decisions then flow from tier to tier. This is not always obvious to the engineers at the bottom. If you ask them who decides what they do, what design specifications will be imposed, or what is good or bad in a system, they rarely can point back to investors and stakeholders. Communicating the overall structure and dependencies in an organization becomes increasingly important as the workers become farther distanced from the actual drivers. In the complex environment of today's engineering workforce with complicated and conflicting software tools, tailored GUIS, unachievable deadlines, and conflicting demands and value systems, it is essential to use simple diagrams such as this to put names, faces, or identities to the factors driving the work. Ask the youngest and newest team members how they get paid, who set priorities for their work, and how they determine what is important. Their answers clarify how far removed they are from the big picture and how isolated they are with many fewer mentor-mentee relationships and fewer internal (more www-based) resources. Not long ago, a young engineer told one of us that a product that had been used for over 40 years could not possibly work. Rather than consult with the engineers responsible for that product or the managers, this individual had simply done a web search. An intern complained our models were not comprehensible within our company because he couldn't find them in a Google search. These people need to learn how to find information and how to communicate, and of course, the subject matter experts need to communicate what they can offer.

We can follow through the top-level blocks: Senior Management, Chair or other directing body (often the corporate board), and Legal Counsels who set the corporate culture driving the corporate climate for the next tier of workers. Each of these has direct and indirect communications as their interfaces drive the behaviors of each group to comply with outside forces. Interpersonal, intergroup, and global communications are how these components are held together, and their capabilities are utilized to create products.

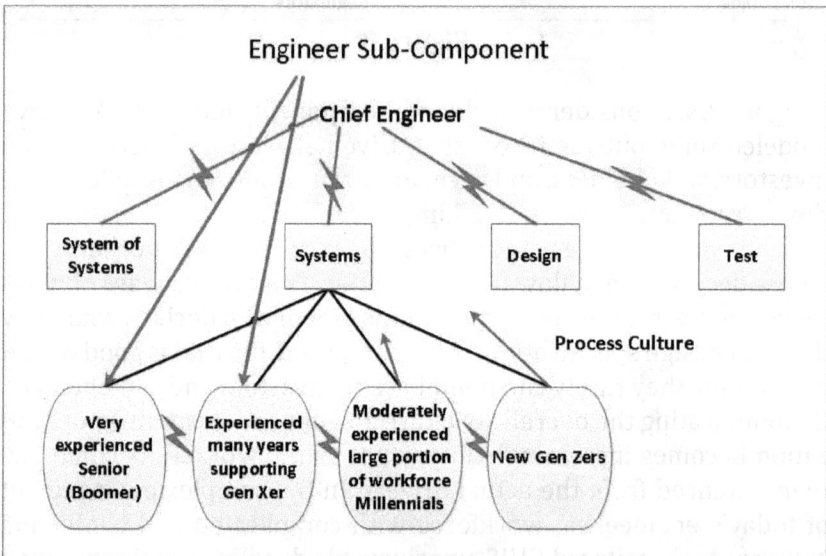

Figure 9

The organization's capabilities are broken down and associated with specific positions, such as the Chief Engineer. The Chief Engineer's work is supported by various engineers, including System of Systems,

Systems, design, and test engineers in this diagram. The Chief Engineer interfaces with each of these through multiple types of communications indicated by the red "lightning bolts."

The communications include, meetings, memorandums and directives, program documents, and there are also engineering software tools that may be configured with specific GUIs to bring the development process into compliance with desired processes. There are informal communications, modeling desired behavior (staying late to complete a project vs going to a movie as planned) in the hallway or via zoom which may be simply a thumbs up or job well done statement. This is one of the areas where our gap analysis indicates the previous systems are breaking down. The communications are not universally understood.

This gap was really the cause for this book, a number of our former customers are asking us to teach their new engineers to think or act like systems engineers while we teach them to write good requirements. To understand where this gap is coming from, we further broke down the Systems Engineering group into 4 tribes of Systems Engineers who are working together to perform the systems engineering function and provide SE capabilities.

There are also dependencies and we have only indicated some that are unique to the current environment and the dependency flowing upward from the Engineering tribes who are driving some of the chief engineer and corporate behaviors.

We have discussed the concept that initially the workforce culture was interpreted by the workforce components via their expressed climate, and they reacted to it in the tribe units however recently the social climate is driving behaviors of some tribes which then press through their climate to change corporate culture. A reversal of previous norms.

We have within the workforce components that are functioning under the previous downwards flow, interpreting culture as communicated through processes, practices, standard and corporate behavior to define their culture. These elements continue to attempt to comply with cultural norms via learned behaviors and set communications.

The newer components imposing their social culture on the corporate climate have different values and beliefs and different behavioral inventories than the others. We also have divisions between functional components such as managers, engineers, and administrators. So, we may have a tribe of bottom-up social and cultural managers and top-down corporate culture complying managers. What ties the two together and allows the disparate workforce components to function together within a program, project, or corporate entity?

The primary interface between these groups is communication; however, it's an area that has been neglected. Communication style and lines have become weak from those whose behavior system naturally avoids verbal communication (many engineers) to those who thrive on dialoguing and dispute (many enterprise architects).

To build an adaptive and reliant workforce, we must create new communication pathways to promote sharing of values, climate, and behaviors from one component to another and allow the flow of culture from societal to corporate to continue in both directions but encompass the disparate workforce elements.

Individuals in the workforce may be divided into tribes or combined as components, or the individual entity may stand. Thus, we may look at Program Managers who have a specific inventory of behaviors and values or simply the function of the program manager.

In older engineering programs of the '60s through the early 90s, development was affected with co-located groups with a common goal. These groups shared an understanding of corporate responsibility and worked together to have on the fly discussions and develop common language and behaviors. Their programs also took a long time, allowing years of discussions and spoken and unspoken conversations to shape their group behaviors and shared understandings; they developed standard ontologies to discuss their ideas and shared everyday society and social culture.

Communications have become more complex as programs speed up and the workforce becomes physically dispersed across societies, cultures, and countries. Sharing a shared vision of successful program goals helped improve communication, but it had begun to have more gaps.

Great, so how do we get better communications? We must start by breaking down the different behavior types within the workplace. There are several options for this type of training, and although we have found the Wiley DiSC program to be closest aligned to our thinking, most of these systems can be adapted to the problem. Rather than focusing on a personality type in isolation, we ask what the communication/personality in the work environment is. Are they analytic, action-based, impulsive, big picture, or highly detailed? This is the essence of the communications portion of our workshops, creating an understanding of the individual. This then is complied with a sense of their generational paradigms and what learning processes they were taught: a few may be left from the progressive era, others held to standardized testing scores, No Child Left Behind, or common core. Each period of education also brought different learning methods combined with the individual innate learning processes.

Each generation also has specific values in terms of work and home life balance, which do conflict across the groups; there are also some demographics creating more significant gaps as few engineers are bridging the gap between "Boomer' and "Millennial" Or even "Generation Z." Each generational period and each learning style and other factors introduce paradigms and value systems however the members of each defined group are individuals. This means they can be sorted into groups with expected behaviors. However, their specific communication pathways will also be determined by their workplace learning type and personality type. We distinguish between life skills and engineering workforce skills, when applying a personality type to how we communicate at work rather than trying to understand ourselves better. We know that different jobs will bring in a concentration of one kind of personality versus another and that the ideal program will have a balance of types. However, the reality is that engineers have fewer outgoing, impulsive fast-twitch thinkers among their numbers; this does help with the communication process. We must rely on those in the social skills fields to train us on how to communicate as an interface between our engineering workforce components and utilize the methods and practices they have so well documented. We then use workshops to tailor these to our specific workplace situations embedded within program or project needs, testing out communications skills to enhance requirements writing or project management planning and sometimes enterprise architecture modeling to get the best impact from acquiring these skills.

8

Applicability of Enterprise Models and Practices

Workforce Resiliency Information Model

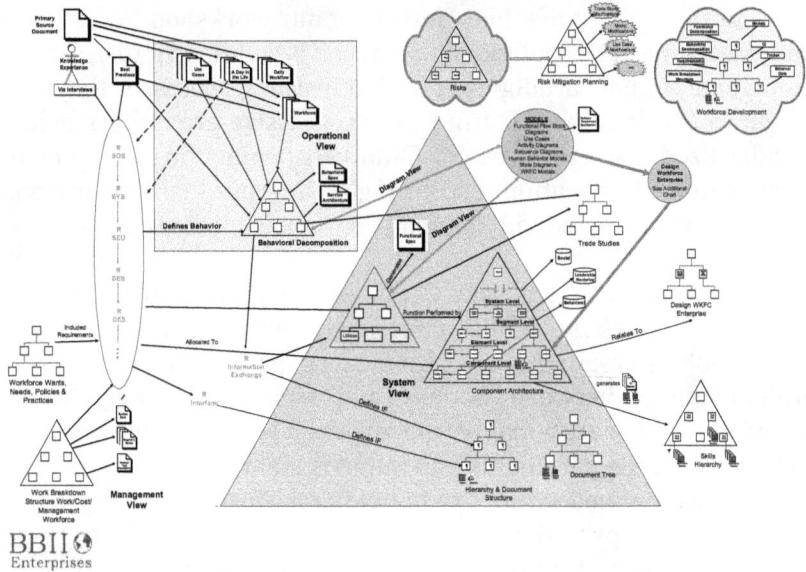

BBII ☺
Enterprises

Figure 10: Enterprise and Systems Engineering Models as Applied to Workforce Paradigms

The Information Model is a tool developed by BBII Enterprise's engineers to capture the elements of any program or organization at the start of a project in order to drive a common understanding of the sources for development, existing infrastructure, and future tool organization. It also includes and defines best processes, practices boundaries and constraints for that undertaking. This model has been modified to drive work force engineering.

Enterprise and systems engineering models are tools used by engineers and architects to handle complexity in originations and programs. The complex elements that comprise an origination and the interfaces between these elements are defined and captured in tools that allow the modeler to examine and develop new products, processes, and behaviors in a multifaceted context. The moving parts, including outside and inside interfaces, required and desired processes, quality measures and metrics, risk analysis, and behaviors rapidly become too numerous and complex to hold in the mind without the aid of models. Those invested in a positive solution, such as the investors or the managers, rely on good models to manage complexity to allow them to evaluate options, impacts and likely outcomes. Models aid in the development of specific focus (mission) and the plans for dissemination of improved processes.

These process improvements and other enterprise changes are needed to create products and services representative of corporate capabilities. For years we have utilized the information models to define program development, drive tool integration, capture processes and practices, and develop EA views and requirements that support program standards of development. The modeling process begins by capturing the sources of information for the program and designating where they flow to and how they are utilized to develop requirements, specifications, milestone documents and to determine what further analysis will be done to ensure a complete set of program documents. Often the model is further broken down to define the engineering tool GUI's to ensure that all the program engineers are working in the same paradigm. Further reviews of model elements can ensure that all of the contributors have completed their task to the necessary level, have they defined their portion of the system sufficiently and included all necessary elements. The model allows space to link documents and requirements to test plans and procedures, proposals, simulations and other development areas. To learn more about using this model to create a knowledge store see (Appendix 1).

For those of who organize program chaos with the information model and other modeling tools, it makes sense to turn to these same modeling tools and modify them for handling the complexity of the demands and gaps in workforce capabilities and development. This allows us to identify the known moving parts, evaluate who and what are impacted by changes and perform gap analysis when considering if we have identified a good intervention to support and retain the engineering workforce as a whole and as individuals.

Workforce engineering models can create a repository to facilitate shared understanding of the complex elements of employee behaviors, communications, values, abilities, and skills that underpin the resilience workshops, and development of skill sets. The shared process of defining these Workforce Enterprise models, with input from the "workforce," is essential if we want to succeed. The process of workshopping or interviewing to gain the information to populate the model is the first step to educate workforce members and train them to support new standards and demands. The next step is to prepare, present and disseminate the models in terms that apply to each group of workers.

Enterprise Architects model the mission, vision, behaviors, and services of an enterprise to facilitate an understanding of how all the elements of an organization function. This expedites development, growth, productive practices, and ensures safety and responsibility of engineers as they develop critical products. Modeling enterprise elements means modeling the "factory" which is the organization that creates products. The modeler breaks down the overall enterprise into the functions, systems, services, and behaviors needed to create a desired product.

In terms of the human element, this means considering the workforce: the people who make the product, the practices they use to produce, the skills they have or need to acquire, and the value and communication systems that guide them as well as the equipment they use modeling the complex factors that make up workforce components allows users to rely on the model and modeling tools to handle all the complicated pieces and parts of the system (or enterprise) to consider the impacts of changes and new ideas. These models allow clear patterns to emerge in valued behaviors and services. The utilization of models in developing new systems is a common and essential practice. The utilization of models in enterprise development is fairly common (and often mandated by government law). However, these models are not commonly adopted into the full workflow. The EA's and SoS (System of Systems) engineers are often put to the side creating models and documents for "compliance" only. They are forced to beg and hunt for their data as the applied engineers continue their work. In these cases, the enterprise modeling process must be brought into the mainstream and treated as the center of the workforce development program rather than an obscure team laboring to get a gold star in compliance tests. In more integrated teams, the value of modeling becomes clear since they can model "what if" and "as if" ideas and changes.

Our experience participating in teams to create knowledge repositories and then to create Knowledge Management systems and the distributed learning systems utilized the EA and Systems models for ongoing development of both the complete program and the specific repositories. Fully defined elements of the models were applied directly to coding and development of the tools and repositories. The model development process has also helped us to recognize the benefits of using modeling tools to capture the human factors within the actual workforce. In the case of the initial knowledge repository simply asking participants what data they collect and what tools they use uncovered data repositories that had been isolated from other users and the resulting frustration of engineers who did not know how to connect this data with those who might need it. Others found that they had specific knowledge (of how test software was used, or where development documents were stored) that needed to be streamlined into program processes. The models in the end defined both data uses. It makes sense to use the same types of models to capture the behaviors and emotions of the workforce elements i.e., the actual people doing the work that make up the enterprise. Incorporating these users in the modeling process drives understanding and reveals consensus of the gaps and strengths of a workforce system. It also allows open communication of value system conflicts. These are further enhanced with two systems, the behavioral and communications skill building further discussed in chapters 7 and 8.

We have found that is essential to select tools and languages that best match the skills of the organization's engineers. There is no perfect tool despite the fact that software tool designers attempt to tailor their tools to different industries; it should be the organization's needs driving the tool, not the tools marketing overlays. I once used a router to cut a diagonal section of my desk, a jigsaw might have been "better" but I had a router and I was very familiar with it. The router is a slower tool for cutting a line but it is faster to us and I am already familiar with it and using it is more efficient than acquiring a new tool and learning how to use it. This metaphor holds true for all the software-based engineering tools, the one you have best learned to bend to your processes is the right one for the job.

Tool selection defines the processes that will be used to collect, store and disseminate the information to be gathered prior to moving on to model development. The model development process includes capturing "as is" and "as was" views of how the organization works (down to the workforce elements components) and developing a desired "to be" view based on what is available. This includes an assessment of what were the political and social environments of the workforce as it had been functioning (perhaps prior to Covid related shutdowns) and the desired changes that need to be made. How the envisioned corporate culture changes will affect these human components and how will they be implemented. For established businesses that had existing business plans, models and perhaps a full Enterprise Architecture model set, access to prepopulated information on the mission and vision, organization structure, past product lines, and services, would offer the Architects a head start in building workforce resilience as existing views can then build basic models to serve as informative workshopping tools.

Practical Workforce Redesign Realities

There are two goals for the workshops: one is to build and assess a downwards flow of information from the organization concerning the mission vision and values to the individuals who make up the workforce. There is also a less direct goal of demonstrating to workers that they are still an essential part of any organization and exist within a structure vs. being considered lone individuals working for money. The second goal is to capture workers' values and uncover the divisions that will guide and form the future organizational structure an enterprise needs to create in order to succeed. There must be compromise between the "as was" and the "to be" views from the top down and bottom up and a unifying force of shared values in order for any enterprise to succeed. This compromise requires interactions between the groups that are facilitated by models but that must also ultimately be expressed by behaviors of both parties.

Addressing and understanding resiliency when facing today's realities is essential. Companies have always needed to constantly adapt to internal and external dynamic market forces. But in these times in order to successfully evolve a company also critically needs to understand individual resiliency and understand how to promote it as an essential aspect of enterprise success. Usually, when the market changes, internal changes are manifested via mandates. But if the supporting workforce resists investing in your proposed changes then process and practice amendments will fail. Therefore the notion and modes of leveraging your workforce must also change with the times. Enterprises may not be able to fire staff that resists, ready replacements aren't always available, and losing corporate knowledge and experience is always a concern. Currently, in many industries, management now faces a worker generation that doesn't respond to that kind of pressure the same way the previous generation did. Being informed about individual emotional, cognitive, mental, physical, and spiritual needs fosters enterprise resiliency and equips management with the tools needed to create a resilient workforce that can and wants to absorb and actively support adaptations management makes to protocols and existing responsibilities. If this dynamic is not addressed at the individual level, then everything we will discuss from now on will not work.

We need new ways to encourage our workforce to invest in even the simplest mandates, (i.e., "show up at 9:00 o'clock sharp not, "leave your house at 9:00 o'clock sharp"). We need to alter individuals' relationships to change. In the past, individuals were concerned they would be fired if they did not do what everyone else did, or all that they were asked to do, but those pressures do not always work today. For better or worse, your workforce has options. So, we need to do some homework. We want workers to readily adapt and engage when responsibilities, processes, and policies shift. We are not done with the raft of marketplace changes the pandemic has advanced. Inflation is our next challenge and source acquisition has become more difficult.

For example, a company that builds film sets and yoga walls, now faces the fact that the wood products it ordered from a private shipper have not been delivered and in fact, are not yet available, but this company is getting new jobs as the entertainment and yoga businesses ramp up again. So now management needs to locate a new source and implement a new delivery protocol immediately. A new source is located but now the wood has been shipped to a consumer warehouse store where it will be set aside for this company's use. However, the materials are being set aside *outside* so now management needs to get staff that is used to working on film sets alone, to drive to Home Depot and package or protect these materials so they won't get destroyed by predicted rainstorms while they wait for transport. In this case, employees responded to this urgent request with, "Well that's not something I do." To solve the immediate problem the company owner drives to North Carolina and oversees the tarping. She has to drive her car because there weren't any rental cars available, and she cannot fly like she used to, and so on. But she has employees who are saying, "Well, that's not my job," and "That's not why you pay me." She needs her staff to develop a more amenable attitude towards new responsibilities and to embrace the idea that she is not arbitrarily forcing these changes but that she is doing it because the marketplace has changed, and her enterprise needs to follow suit to survive. She needs to change how she communicates her reasons. Her message needs to be more inclusive. She also needs to understand the shift in focus from being a cog in the machinery of an impersonal business team to being a personal player in a specific role that supports an integrated team.

"I hear you. You want to go to the job site and be there all day and do your job and go home. You do not want to drive to two different locations. But I am asking you to do something different because new market forces have exposed *us*, and we need to do more than just build sets for now."

In this example, the workforce has to trust their CEO and her enterprise. They need to believe that *she understands* their concerns, but that they have to compromise to succeed. She needs to use different behaviors and her organization needs some resilience inserted into the system to encourage and speed up the pace of adaptation. This business owner found different ways to get the wood, but her enterprise lacked the trustworthy dynamic connection between management and staff needed to get the two entities to move forward together. She needs to overcome that obstacle in order to achieve success.

The point of view from staff is that in the old days when employees joined a company, they would work incredible hours in the beginning because they lacked the expertise and experience they would gain.

Over time, as they became more senior employees, they would not have to work those extraordinary hours once they acquired expertise, i.e., the ability to cover responsibilities that time and experience on the job had helped them develop. They believed that if they worked hard and went the extra mile, i.e., did things like going to the Home Depot and tarping the wood, there would be a long-term benefit, a lifetime job. They valued the job, and they worked for a company that ensured its employees had jobs. But now employees cannot count on that kind of security, and they do not trust that management is invested enough in their well-being that they can still say, "Alright if this is what you need, then I'm willing to do it because I understand we're in it together."

Resilience includes the notion of rebuilding a lost sense of community. We create enterprise architecture models. We capture the best practices, and we get the best processes idea. We've done all that, but we need to rebuild the bridge between us the workforce and us the enterprise so that workforce members feel safe adjusting to changes in terms of what has to be accomplished so that they wholly support the enterprise and even become invested in finding enterprise solutions.

Constantly Evolving Economic Realities

Enterprises adapt to market forces by understanding their strengths and weaknesses as they adapt to new marketplace demands. We think of these things already. Documented in George Kozmetsky's: "Zero Time Management," for example, Zero-Time management unites the innovator, affective producer, and relationship manager aspects of economic success in a manner that allows organizations to anticipate change and provide value for stakeholders immediately. The theory focuses on five basic concepts, "Instant Value Alignment" with customers, "Instant Learning" by employees and customers, "Instant Adaptation" of the organization, "Instant Execution" of value for the customer, and "Instant Involvement" of all stakeholders. An example of this in action is locating an unfulfilled customer opportunity, developing a key core competency to exploit that opportunity, and expanding into zero-time operations. In other words, applying your vision, core competence, and distinctiveness for one market and expanding into different but similar (adjacent) markets.

We already address issues such as: What does my enterprise do? What capabilities does my organization already have? What are the business spaces adjacent to (or similar to) the ones currently supplied by the company/organization? How would the business move into these new areas?

BBII Enterprises and our supporting team members teach workforce resiliency which is adjacent to teaching systems engineering and enterprise architecture because in recent years there is less demand for systems engineering and enterprise architecture training, so we adjusted by teaching this same workforce we already have in training, to be adaptable and resilient. We recognized that there were more urgent novel market needs than building new airplanes. Our clients need to inculcate adaptability and resiliency into the workplaces and so we retooled to train new skill sets. That's what a successful enterprise must do. The market forces enterprises to develop new modes of success. The stage building company had to adapt to a rupture in its supply chain. It found new suppliers and agreed to collect the wood from another state at Home Depot. It hired truckers and agreed to several, instead of one, delivery sites and accepted the responsibility of toting the wood home itself. And it accepted the task of protecting raw materials from the rain. This company is going to meet its customers' demand by matching the shifts in the supply chain so that it can keep making products by using different types of models that will help it be ready for the next change as they forecast for marketplace uncertainty. It now also needs to ensure its workforce members are invested in the changes and it needs the other enterprises with which it interacts to trust the changes it is making.

Buyers and cooperative enterprises will buy from you or move on. A bread maker needs to know how many loaves of bread he can sell and trade it against how much it costs him to scale up or scale down to meet the market need to keep all his stakeholders satisfied. These are things that every successful enterprise understands.

Enterprises can also fail because the individual member (or governing board or individual) believes he/she/they are too big or good to fail. In short, they think they can't. This is a result of remaining loyal to an obsolete standard of success. DEK computers once were the biggest and the best, can't fail, mainframe computers with billboards and buildings all over Boston. Have you seen a DEK computer in 20 years?

DEK provided the big corporate computers. They were huge and they owned a chunk of the Boston economy. They kept making computers bigger and more expensive, but they were the kinds of computers that lived in a room with an air conditioner. DEK failed to adapt their business models to the advent of and demand for the PC revolution (individually oriented personal computers) and so they did not adapt, and they died.

Polaroid offered one type of technology. Everyone wanted it because there was nothing else like it, but they failed to notice the advent of the digital age. When customers didn't want Polaroid photos anymore because there were better options, Polaroid didn't adapt, and it died. Kodak suffered as well and is currently at risk of suffering the same fate for the same reason. But it has managed to stay competitive by selling digital cameras, printers, and printing paper.

Enterprises need to notice change, notice it quickly, and adapt quickly without having to learn something completely new. Change is occurring at a more rapid pace than ever before. There is a lot of instability in the market right now. Businesses and organizations are all going to have to try this, and try that, turn right, maybe turn left. There will be mistakes, but we shouldn't be afraid of that if we foster the ability to shift gears and perspectives quickly. "Yes, I hired you to do one thing and now I need you to do another." You need a secure workforce that has enough trust and enough capability to propel the business (enterprise?) into the adjacent business spaces to their current product lines in order to keep your enterprise afloat and in order to benefit from new opportunities that benefit individual members of your company and your enterprise as a whole.

This is especially critical now after people have experienced a long moment in which they've all felt incredibly harassed by a number of disasters on all fronts. They have less trust in authority figures and feel less able to recover from more changes. They also feel overwhelmed by messaging, are they safe or at risk, is returning to work a good social support or a scientific death sentence, or do they have to live in the uncomfortable and complicated in between? An employee working for a computer management consultant company recently quit her job. She had weathered a tough set of years. In addition to enduring the quarantine and surviving the economic downturn, she had experienced a personal disaster. Her house burned down, and she found herself engaged in a war with both the government and her insurance company when she attempted to rebuild. This caused discord in her marriage. It all added up. Now when she is not feeling at all resilient after suffering all these changes in her private life, she certainly does not feel ready to make more adjustments or more sacrifices at work.

Enterprises need to understand how complicated and confusing the work is right now and how that can conflict and obfuscate corporate and individual loyalty and values. When all is confusing, depressing, and scary, people grab for certainty even when they are divisive, tribal, or wrong. Enterprise managers need to support their workforce so that it is resilient enough to ride through the changes the organization must make and will need to make in the future in a timely manner. Enterprises cannot move their production into the adjacent space and cannot make rapid course corrections for changes in supply chains if they don't bring their workforce along with them in the decision-making process. Business leaders don't want to complicate your employees' personal lives and the workplace is not a place for therapy, but in a human and productive sense, unless the workplace helps the workforce to deal with the emotional cost of the past year and the toll it has taken on its employees, it will not succeed.

Understanding Enterprise Value Systems

We have already discussed the generational forces altering the workforce value system, but there are other factors driving the need to change. These include a multitude of health scares, the immediate effect of an environment altered by COVID-19, disinformation, disharmonious politics, and a long bailout period in which people had to decide whether to pay rent *and how*. Some got handouts that can't go on forever. People are nervous about returning to an uncertain workforce situation and fearful of leaving the safety of their homes where they have been propped up and supported. As we enter into the next phase, which could include hyperinflation and a collapse of markets, individual and enterprise resilience is going to matter even more. You are returning to work, but how secure is the salary situation? Will it be enough if inflation rolls on in? How will you buy your groceries? And that's what is coming next. If we want to survive and thrive, we must adapt and hope to develop new solutions, which might come from a more secure workforce. Maybe an organization is going to have to buy your groceries. We don't know. We don't know what will happen next, but we do know that that's why we need to train and teach and learn resilience

Enterprise value systems are linked to what services and products organizations offer; they answer questions as to what good business ideas and bad business ideas are. Value systems relate to quality and qualify how an organization assesses that. Apple values new and interesting technology, often at the expense of reliability. They distribute products that do not entirely work but are sparkling new and can accept system updates. An aircraft propulsion system manufacturer values repeatability and reliability above all else. If I have a new idea for an application, I would not bring it to businesses with high reliability and expensive testing requirements such as Pratt and Whitney or Bombardier, I would take it to Apple instead because Apple values innovative new approaches and exciting new technology but Pratt and Whitney, Bombardier, Lockheed, or Boeing prioritize values differently and with good reason. It has to do with the product they are developing and the clients they need to satisfy.

In terms of the workforce then enterprises want workers to adopt and support their specific value systems. Thus, management needs to know what they are and be able to articulate them and communicate them to workers who did not grow up in the existing workforce and who don't know what the values are or that they may change over time.

"Can you believe Brooks Brothers failed," "Boeing is in the news because of software failures." In each of these cases brand new technology was brought in, fielded, and determined to be unreliable and failed the enterprises in which reliability is more critical than innovation. The organizations themselves did not know what they wanted or needed. Furthermore, because we are often attached to the idea that big established organizations cannot fail, often the failure begins within a workforce that doesn't understand that their new solutions will fail because they assumed success and didn't speak out when it was clear that the new ideas weren't workable, to start.

Different enterprises have different value systems which require different behaviors in terms of the workforce and of product assessment. If a workforce does not understand the enterprise's value system, it won't assess potential solutions properly. A recent customer claim is: "We want emergent systems. We want everybody working for us to suggest something new that we can make that will be better than whatever we already have." But this logic is based on the assumption that newly designed products will work on a 40-year-old submarine. When the new product, idea, or process failed this client it was, in part, because the customer did not demonstrate an understanding of its actual value system or the parts of an old system they intend to keep when they rally around the idea of innovation. This organization does not actually desire or value emergent systems, it values very reliable, maintainable, implementable systems that are the same as or incrementally better, than the ones they already have that demonstrate low failure rates. They may wish for more modern technology, but they don't actually want systems that change quickly and might actually adapt as they are used. Miscommunication usually begins within an enterprise and then infects the interaction between enterprises. We worked with a company that developed training systems to sell to a military group. This enterprise wanted training games. They had seen the rising popularity of the games and liked them because they were exciting and used realistic military assets. Game scenarios included helicopters and ground vehicles that were modeled after the army's helicopter and ground assets. This enterprise saw that people love playing the games because they offered realistic experiences. It was believed that the new products would engage trainees more effectively. Stated value systems included creating new gaming products that could be offered in the commercial arena as well, that could be reconfigured on a whim, that were cheaper and flashier and thus more appealing to kids coming out of high school and enlisting. The fatal design flaw was a lack of actual realism in terms of battle tactics. A ground force vehicle is a huge tank that can transport a small platoon or half of a platoon. It looked real in the game. But the point of the training was to practice joint tactics and joint operations in the field. In the game, the scenarios invented to demonstrate the vehicle's usefulness failed to consider essential real world, real combat issues, and environmental concerns that affect how soldiers behaved and needed to behave in order to ensure that the most secure strategies were utilized. The customer was as a result upset because the game was unrealistic in this sense. They wanted a game that prioritized experiences they knew their soldiers would have to face. They valued realism over the qualities they listed when they initially said they wanted an engaging, commercial, inexpensive, and easily configurable training game, but in the end, they valued something contrary to their ask which led to failure.

In terms of enterprise architecture, the first task is to work with an enterprise to develop an understanding of the values that actually drive it and second, to understand how to adapt when the values change (or are not addressed) and to quickly determine what need to change as a result and then to communicate these ideas to the workforce so it will invest and adapt as well. The above example is one in which both tasks were ignored.

Our team knows how to help enterprises understand what value systems are and how they need to be communicated to the workforce and how that works to alter the process. If someone has an idea, to create color instead of a black and white image, you need to know if that change is important to you or not and what you are willing to sacrifice as a result. If a new venture is begun that changes needs for skills and staffing, does the organization intend to save all your employees? Is the better plan to do it cheaper or is something else more important? Your workforce needs to understand the what's and the why's as well. When an enterprise changes values it communicates these changes through models and tools that flow into changing processes, practices, and management, and that works great as long as you have the resilient workforce to absorb those changes and that can do something with this information besides resist.

"No, I'm not coming into work."

"No, I'm not going to go tarp that wood because these are not the things that I do."

As individuals on the team and at BBII, having spent most of our careers working with enterprises and with the individuals making products the way enterprises want, we can see that the tool that's lacking isn't: how do I write a good requirement, or how do I write a good code. But how do I adapt to the changes that are going to make me write that better or understand the need more, and that's why we're here to help you change that.

We need to understand our existing capabilities and learn how to use what we already know well to expand into these adjacent areas. BBII teaches workforce resiliency using systems engineering principles. We already knew how to organize workshops for engineers using SOS principles. When we needed to include new principles in this paradigm, i.e., resiliency. We created an adjacent space utilizing skills and knowledge we had already mastered. We understand what we're doing, and we also see the differences that need to be made to meet new market needs in order for us to survive.

Say we were rock climbers. Someone might say "You know how to rock climb so why not build a business that teaches these skills?" Teaching rock climbing is not adjacent to what we're doing when we climb as a hobby. We like to rock climb but other than that it's not the next slot over in terms of our capabilities. We have to be able to teach rock climbing. We have to understand liability issues. We need to know what the marketplace for rock climbing is and what the regulations are for engaging in such an enterprise. There are many capabilities we would have to learn to make this shift which needs to be made in terms of Zero Time management and its linkage with resilient systems engineering principles and developing a resilient workforce.

We seek to make the logical move with the capabilities we have and develop those we don't very quickly. Zero Time management is about the ability to anticipate where the market is going and the ability to know yourself well enough to understand what part of that open space you can take on and what part you cannot. Back to the rock climber example, we could teach the skill set but we can't just slide over and start teaching it tomorrow and be successful if we don't reevaluate our capacity to meet the new needs on a real level. We need to know our capabilities and our value systems. This means not just assuming them but learning to demonstrate an explicit understanding of these specifics. Many companies don't know their expertise or their values, they assume them. Enterprise and systems engineering are important in this resiliency process if you want to flex into a new business space. You need to know the value of your company when you're doing something different and that again falls under this Zero Time behavior creating an enterprise that is elastic and resilient because it can move into adjacent spaces but only if the systems engineering and enterprise architecture principles are completed. And this will only occur if we know who they are and what they can do.

It is critical to understand what our core capabilities are and to know that our workforce understands them and understands that we're adapting and changing even when it comes to support of the workforce. How much of the workforce can and should work remotely? Does it impact core capabilities, are training and mentoring moments lost, is trust lost, are transactions handled securely, and is there a clear path for feedback and follow up. Is animal daycare a new need? Should we consider it or is it an unworkable proposal? We need to understand what and where we can flex and where we can't. Tons of animals were adopted during this stay-at-home COVID so this is now an issue. Pet owners don't want to return to work because of their pets.

Returning to the essential models at the start of this chapter, if they have been developed then the business leaders will know what the core values, essential capabilities, services, and behaviors of their organizations are. Within the systems engineering enterprise, they can evaluate whether to support that problem or learn where the adjustments need to be made and lean on new skills of listening, feedback and compromise to support their workforce and rebuild a cohesive effort. And they can also begin to include the workforce core values, concerns, and behaviors that have been altered by recent events as part of the modeling process increasing the ability to evolve and inculcating these workforce concerns into successful protocols rather than defining them as obstacles to success.

References

Amiama-Espaillat, C., & Mayor-Ruiz, C. (2017). Digital reading and reading competence. The influence in the Z generation from the Dominican Republic. *Comunicar*, 25(52), 105-114. https://doi.org/10.3916/c52-2017-10.

Beck, Aaron T. (1996). Cognitive therapy and emotional disorders. Penguin Random House.

Bolton, Patrick Bolton. CEA, TOGAF, Zachman Practice Leader for Management | Business Consulting, Integrated Systems, Inc. Founding faculty and instructor of the FEAC Institute and TO-GAF.

Bonanno, G. A. (2021). *The End of Trauma: How the New Science of Resilience is Changing How We Understand PTSD*. Basic Books.

Borchers, C. (2022, February 24). Sorry, Bosses: Workers Are Just Not That Into You. WSJ. https://www.wsj.com/articles/why-workers-not-back-to-office-bosses-11645640418

Context, Conditions, and Culture. (2021, July 7). *Harvard Business Review*. *https://hbr.org/2018/01/context-conditions-and-culture?ab=seriesnav-spotlight*

COVID-19: Implications for business. (2022, April 13). McKinsey & Company. Retrieved April 30, 2022, from https://www.mckinsey.com/business-functions/risk-and-resilience/our-insights/covid-19-implications-for-business

Dey, M. (2020, June 24). *Ability to work from home: evidence from two surveys and implications for the labor market in the COVID-19 pandemic: Monthly Labor Review: U.S. Bureau of Labor Statistics*. U.S. Bureau of Statistics. Retrieved July 16, 2021, from https://www.bls.gov/opub/mlr/2020/article/ability-to-work-from-home.htm

Employers, employees less optimistic about finances in 2013. (2013, June 1). Benefits Pro. Retrieved July 15, 2022, from https://www.benefitspro.com/2013/01/16/employers-employees-less-optimistic-about-finances/?slreturn=20220330155510

Engler, H. (2020, March 23). *Covid-19: Employee behavioral risks rise as covid-19 lockdown fuels performance pressure.* JD Supra. Retrieved August 17, 2021, from https://www.jdsupra.com/legalnews/covid-19-employee-behavioral-risks-rise-45712/

Fry, R. (2021, May 28). *Millennials overtake Baby Boomers as America's largest generation.* Pew Research Center. Retrieved June 15, 2021, from https://www.pewresearch.org/fact-tank/2020/04/28/millennials-overtake-baby-boomers-as-americas-largest-generation/

Gallo, G. (2021). Conflict theory, complexity and systems approach. *Systems Research and Behavioral Science, 30*(2), 156–175. https://doi.org/10.1002/sres.2132

Gordon, G. (2020, July 4). *High-risk, low-frequency events in public safety.* Lexipol. Retrieved May 26, 2022, from https://www.lexipol.com/resources/blog/high-risk-low-frequency-events-in-public-safety/

How Businesses Have Successfully Pivoted During the Pandemic. (2021, February 2). Harvard Business Review. Retrieved April 30, 2021, from https://hbr.org/2020/07/how-businesses-have-successfully-pivoted-during-the-pandemic

Intermittent social distancing may be needed through 2022 to manage covid-19 2022. Retrieved April 30, 2022, from https://www.hsph.harvard.edu/news/hsph-in-the-news/intermittent-social-distancing-may-be-needed-through-2022-to-manage-covid-19/

Kochhar, R., & Bennett, J. (2021, April 14). *U.S. labor market inches back from the COVID-19 shock, but recovery is far from complete.* Pew Research Center. Retrieved June 6, 2021, from https://www.pewresearch.org/fact-tank/2021/04/14/u-s-labor-market-inches-back-from-the-covid-19-shock-but-recovery-is-far-from-complete/

NASA. (2015, May 13). *Newton's third law of Motion.* NASA. Retrieved February 24, 2022, from https://www.grc.nasa.gov/www/k-12/rocket/newton3r.html.

OECD (2021), *OECD Science, Technology and Innovation Outlook 2021: Times of Crisis and Opportunity,* OECD Publishing, Paris, https://doi.org/10.1787/75f79015-en.

Parker, K., & Igielnik, R. (2022, April 1). On the Cusp of Adulthood and Facing an Uncertain Future: What We Know About Gen Z So Far. Pew Research Center's Social & Demographic Trends Project. https://www.pewresearch.org/social-trends/2020/05/14/on-the-cusp-of-adulthood-and-facing-an-uncertain-future-what-we-know-about-gen-z-so-far-2/

Parker, K., Igielnik, R., & Kochhar, R. (2021, February 10). *Unemployed Americans are feeling the emotional strain of job loss; most have considered changing occupations.* Pew Research Center. Retrieved December 7, 2022, from https://www.pewresearch.org/fact-tank/2021/02/10/unemployed-americans-are-feeling-the-emotional-strain-of-job-loss-most-have-considered-changing-occupations/

Pettigrew, Andrew M. (1979). Qualitative Methodology. Administrative Science Quarterly, 24(4), 707–711. https://doi.org/10.2307/2392363.

R. (2021, March 19). *The OODA Loop: How Fighter Pilots Make Fast and Accurate Decisions.* Farnam Street. https://fs.blog/ooda-loop/

Rao, Prakesh C., Reedy, Ann, Bellman, Beryl. (2019). All in One Enterprise Architecture Exam Guide. EBOOKREADING.NET. Retrieved January 23, 2022, from https://ebookreading.net/view/book/EB9781260121490_3.html.

Russell, Bertrand. (2004). *Power: A New Social Analysis*. Routledge. Source: https://quotepark.com/quotes/1844647-bertrand-russell-power-may-be-defined-as-the-production-of-intended/

Seemiller, C., & Grace, M. (2016). *Generation Z Goes to College*. Jossey-Bass.

Thomas, I. (2022, March 4). *Big February job growth for economy, but on Main Street it's still a struggle to find workers*. CNBC. https://www.cnbc.com/2022/03/04/even-with-job-gains-small-businesses-are-struggling-to-hire-workers.html.

Appendix 1

How to Create an Information Model and Roadmap for Workforce Development Knowledge Base

The goals are to increase communication across different groups and to capture information flow first in diagrams and then in a data store such as Apache Hadoop or Cassandra etc., that is organized and driven by the Information Model.

It is helpful to include in this process communications and behavioral workshops. These allow individuals to identify their communication "style" or "type" at work in order to learn how best to communicate with others of different styles. This promotes the information gathering process, increases understanding and balance (resilience) across the different groups and can better inform the index or GUI making process to ensure that the knowledge base is intuitively accessible to all the users. Sometimes this is not immediately accessible, often this type of "overhead" or "research" work is forced into the margins in which case we can begin with the understanding we have and attempt to integrate the communication workshops as the knowledge base is socialized across the organization.

Step 1: Make a draft of where the organization n is and where it wants to be. Create a notional timeline for the different elements that must change. This will be your roadmap. We have utilized UML 1.0 swim lanes for this task in the past, but we have also used Gantt charts. Your swim lanes are likely to be different than the ones here as you will be concentrating on personal skills and communications; however, they are still interdependent on other elements of the organization and there is an end product for the organization not just "better skills"

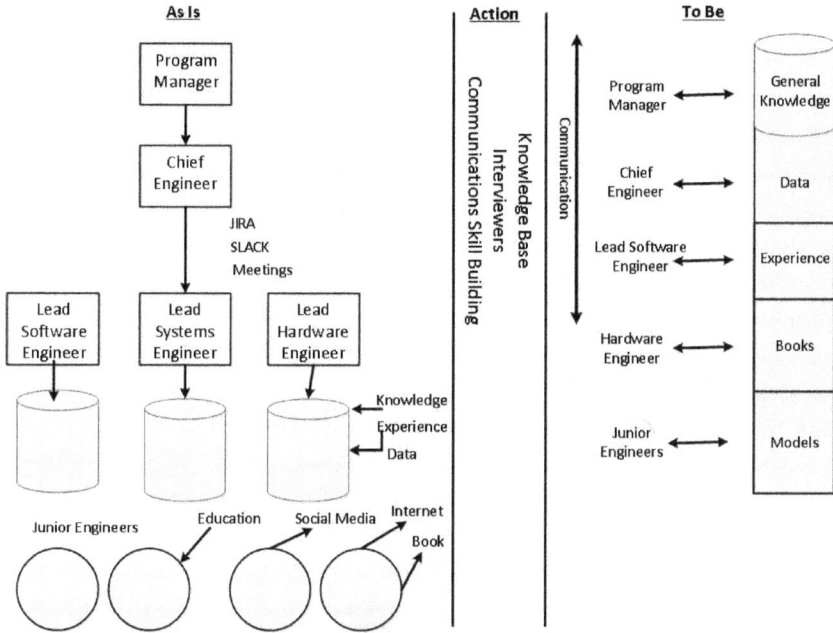

Figure 11

Step 2: Evaluate the resources - who is available to collect information, can you utilize new hires or younger workers who will get better informed about the environment

Step 3: Who are the repositories of knowledge? Use org charts, HR knowledge it is no longer a question of walking the floors since everyone is distributed and virtual. Instead, it is required of the individuals to ask managers and leads (who has been around for a while)? Team leads? Software experts? Who represents the test group? Try to find representatives from each area of information and then use them to populate a draft organization chart. The goal is to identify relationships and hierarchies to see how influence and information flow across the organization.

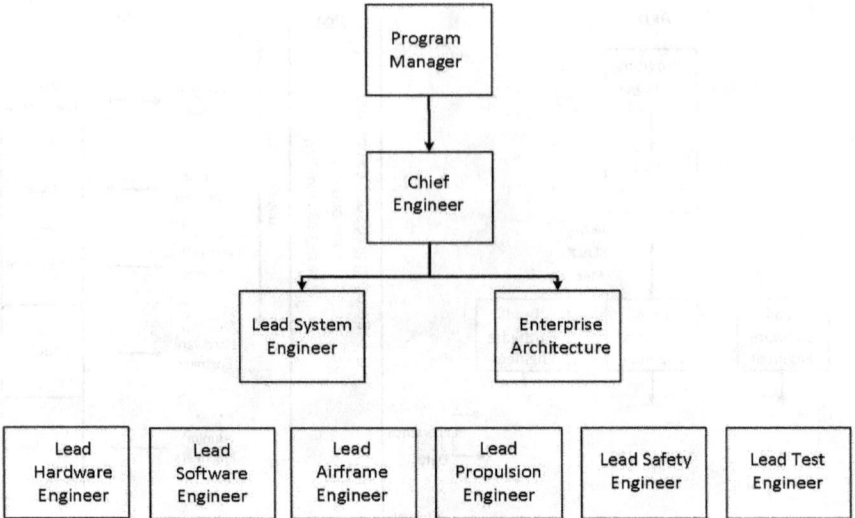

Figure 12

Step 4: develop a questionnaire to find out what each person does, what data they collect, who they communicate with, and how processes and improvements trickle down to them or fail to. Interview to see if they feel that they are part of a team or solitary workers. What tools do they use? What expertise do they have aside from their job description? Are they experts in old CAD drawings? Have they kept performance data in a desk drawer? Are they familiar with human factors considerations in design?

A wide array of questions need to be asked to elicit the true gems of from participants. It is also important to find out how they communicate with the rest of the organization and what gaps and frustrations they may have. In one of these interview processes I found out that all the performance data for a test bed was kept and carefully maintained in a drawer because the display boards had been taken down ten years before and no alternatives had been supplied. The person responsible for this used to participate in monthly lunch sessions where data was exchanged but those meetings were no longer held. It was during the interview process that I discovered this person was collecting and generating important data sets and storing them in a drawer.

Later in my career, I found some newer hires working in a very partitioned and isolated program who were going through documents in a file cabinet because they did not know where else to retrieve data. This time the organization chart was one of the first steps followed by a tour of the facilities to find labs and other locations where these new employees could connect with other people. Perhaps a virtual tour could be arranged with different groups presenting summaries of their work on a series of virtual meetings.

SAMPLE: Your Organization Interview Form

Date ____

Interview Participant's Name.

What is your job title? / How long have you been in your present position?

What is your organization title and identifier (what group do you work for)?

Describe your job function.

Describe the function of your directorate/branch.

Do you have access to guidelines/processes on how to coordinate/perform the primary objective on your job?

Are the functions in <u>your</u> discipline dependent on <u>other</u> disciplines?

What are the functions? In addition, what disciplines do you depend on to achieve the primary objectives of your discipline?

Are there any documented guidelines/process on what the inter-dependencies are between your code (discipline) and other codes (disciplines) during a project lifecycle?

If not, would you find this information helpful? See above).

Are there functions pertaining to your branch/directorate which are dependent on other branches/directorates?

What are these functions and what are the branches/directorates you are dependent on to achieve your primary objectives?

Are there any documented guidelines/process on how to interface between the inter-dependencies in your branch/directorate and other branches / directorates?

If not, would you find this information helpful?

How did you learn the responsibilities and tasks of your present position (a trainer, a training procedure, documentation, previous education and job experience)?

What have you learned since you have been in this job that increases both your productivity and those of the people on your work?

Are there other skills or experience that you would like to make known?

Do you have a clear chain of command?

Do you have a clear organizational chart?

In you have a question or concern are you able to contact the people on this chart directly or indirectly? If not, why not?

Step 4: Create an information model that identifies where data is kept including data and information in key personnel's heads. This model may be drawn in almost any tool, UML or SySML tools may be helpful although MS Visio or MS PowerPoint may be sufficient. The goal is to lay out the information so that it can be communicated back to the other members of the workforce to ensure the flows are both correct and the connections are intuitive.

Step 5: It is beyond the scope of this book to teach how to create a Big Data Knowledge Store. The store design can be guided in part or in great detail by the information model which will be further broken-down form the story telling mode to specific behavior components that describe how the store and data are to be created.

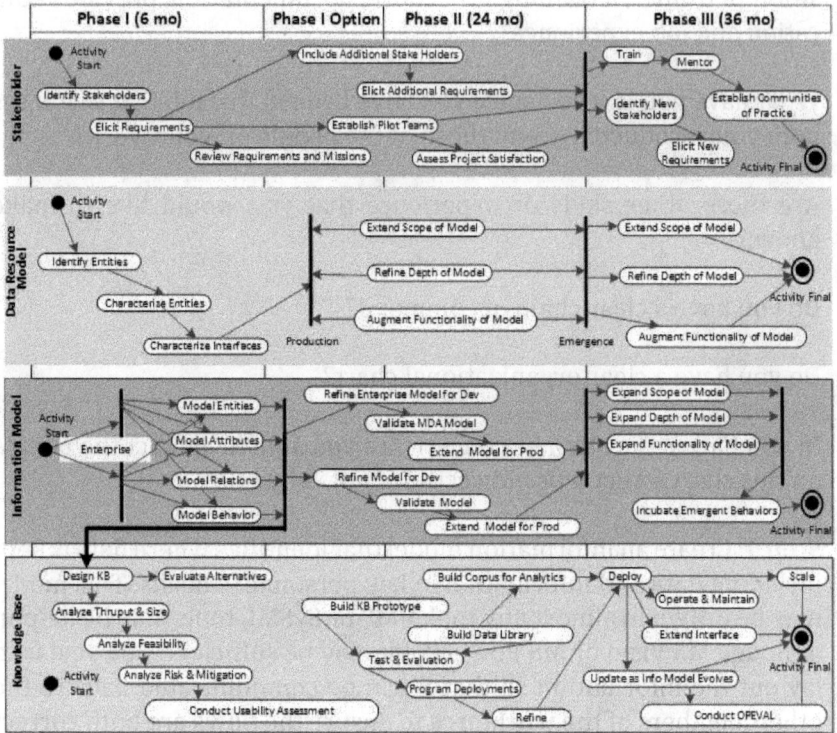

Swim lanes have interconnection relationships which are not shown for clarity – Timeline is not to scale

Index